THE *real* SEX

KITTEN'S

HANDBOOK

THE *real* SEX

KITTEN'S

HANDBOOK

VAL SAMPSON

ILLUSTRATIONS BY PAUL OAKLEY

QUADRILLE

EDITORIAL DIRECTOR Jane O'Shea
ART DIRECTOR Helen Lewis
EDITOR Mary Davies
EDITORIAL ASSISTANT Laura Herring
PRODUCTION Rebecca Short

First published in 2005 by Quadrille Publishing Limited
Alhambra House
27–31 Charing Cross Road
London WC2H 0LS

Cataloguing-in-Publication Data: a catalogue record for this book is
available from the British Library.

ISBN 1 84400 158 X

To Gweneth

For her passion for life
For her commitment to friendship
For her love of lipstick

In all ways an inspiration

Contents

Introduction

Visit any bookstore these days and you'll find almost as many sex books as there are positions in the *Kama Sutra*. *The Real Sex Kitten's Handbook* is fundamentally different from all of them. Why? Because it is a book about sex from a woman's point of view.

Millions of women have been sold the lie that in order to have a great sex life you just have to act more like a man. It's why practically every sex manual ever written focuses on the primarily male preoccupations of technique, position and measuring success by the number of orgasms achieved. Of course, there's nothing wrong with addressing these issues. But it's a little like buying a pair of shoes because they are your size, and you like the colour, *without actually trying them on*. In other words, looking just at the techniques of sex, without examining the feelings of the individuals and the fit of their relationship, is ultimately an empty and wasteful process. Yes, positions and techniques matter, but if they were the certain route to a brilliant sex life there wouldn't be any women around feeling bored and disenchanted with sex. And, sadly, that's just how countless women do feel.

This book offers a different perspective. It is a guide to feeling good about sex as a woman. Because a Sex Kitten knows more than how to turn on her man: she knows how her own sexuality works too. And she recognizes there is more to sex than the male sprint towards orgasm, with her keeping up as best she can. She understands that sex is also about sensuality, and she has the skills to draw her partner into this richer and more rewarding place.

Being a *real* Sex Kitten, by the way, isn't about conforming to a male stereotype: it's about being aware of your sexual power as a woman, and understanding how to use that power to benefit you *and* your partner. It's about feeling sexy in your own skin, and being in touch with your powers of seduction. It is not about physical image – it's a state of mind. You don't need to go on a diet, dye your hair blonde or get a facelift. And exploring your femininity doesn't mean having to be a submissive doormat, any more than a man who is aware of his masculinity has to be a chest-beating Tarzan.

To be truly feminine is to feel powerful and secure in your body. Sex Kittens are confident in their sexuality and themselves ... and nothing is sexier than confidence. So *The Real Sex Kitten's Handbook* won't tell you how to get a man by 'trapping' him with feminine wiles. Instead, it will show you how to feel so good about yourself that all your relationships – with men and women – blossom. It won't illustrate sexual positions in graphic detail, but it will give you explicit information about building intimacy and connection when you make love with your partner. And it will offer easy, straightforward suggestions for getting back into the Sex Kitten groove, or finding it for the first time if you feel it simply passed you by. Because real Sex Kittens get sexier as they grow older.

The Real Sex Kitten's Handbook offers a new approach to sex, an approach based on playfulness, a sense of adventure and a commitment to fun and pleasure. It is a girly book in the very best sense of the word: a celebration of being female, and an acknowledgement that women deserve to experience all of the joys that can bring.

Getting a
sexy mind

Ways to wake up your wild side

The biggest sexual organ in your body is your brain. Unlike the majority of men, who are turned on by what they see, most women are sexually aroused by what they hear and think. That's why the big pharmaceutical companies' search for a female Viagra has virtually ground to a halt. They have discovered something that every Sex Kitten knows: if a woman is to have a memorable sexual experience, she requires more than physical arousal. She needs to be stirred mentally as well as physically. Add emotion to the mix and you have a combination that can't be condensed into a little pink pill.

The chances are that when you meet a new partner you have to make no effort at all to get a sexy mind. In fact, it's practically impossible to get him out of your mind and – if things are really hot – out of your bed. This is because your body goes into hormonal overdrive in the early stages of a relationship. You secrete a hormone, phenylethylamine (PEA), which is an important ingredient in a chemical cocktail that creates a natural high. So the sky seems bluer, the sunshine brighter and chocolate cake even more delicious. It is this hormonal surge that bonds you, so you thrill to your partner's touch and your tummy turns somersaults when he kisses you. ('Teenage' love can strike at any age, by the way. It's perfectly possible to meet a new man at sixty and still quiver inside in exactly the same way that you did at sixteen.)

In the average relationship, this heady, romantic experience usually lasts between three and six exciting months – up to eighteen months for some couples. And then it is replaced by a more realistic approach to each other, as you accept that perhaps your partner is not perfect after all. You may even start to find some of his habits slightly annoying. His previously charming sense of spontaneity can begin to feel like reluctance to make plans. Or the routines that once made him seem so impressive and in control may become slightly constricting. Now, this may not signal the end of the relationship, but it does flag up the fact that you need to talk. And some changes need to be made if the relationship is to stay on track.

This can be a critical moment for a lot of women in their approach to sex. When they discover that their brain is no longer naturally filled with loving and sexy thoughts towards their partner, they go off the idea of making love. They exchange slinky nightwear for comfy pyjamas, or a baggy tracksuit and slippers. Instead of buying a flirty pair of heels and sexy stockings, they opt for trainers and ankle socks. The silky suspenders and wisp of chiffon that once made up their favourite seduction kit are stuffed at the back of the bedroom drawer, and they shut down on thinking about themselves as sensual, sexual beings.

If, by the way, you've always assumed that dressing up for sex in satins and silks is purely about titillating men, it's time for a rethink. Of course, plenty of women enjoy an appreciative male response to clothes that draw attention to smooth skin and soft curves, but it's worth bearing in mind that female skin is around ten times more sensitive than that of the average man. So wearing anything that brushes pleasurably against your body pays dividends for you as well as your partner. By dressing in fabrics that caress your skin, you are helping to wake up your sense of touch and that will heighten your sexual experience later on ...

♥ *Keeping that loving feeling*

Getting a sexy mind requires a degree of determination once the love chemicals begin to fade. Sex Kittens know that they need to carry on doing sexy things, whether it's dressing up for themselves and their partners, say, or planning a surprise seduction after work, in order to keep their minds and bodies feeling sexy. They understand that the romantic pangs and lust of the early days are just a brief stage in the gradual unfolding of a relationship. And that with patience, love and only a little effort on both sides, their relationships are capable of reaching even greater heights of passion as time goes by. So, with this new understanding of how sexual relationships work, try waking up your sexy mind.

FIVE TIPS FOR A SEXY MIND

1. Never underestimate the seductive power of the written word.
One study showed that women who read romantic fiction have better sex lives than women who don't. So, if you've ever felt sorry for the old lady clutching her Mills & Boon, you may be wasting your sympathy.

The joy of a fantasy
is that you don't have
to be responsible,
sensible or
practise safe sex.

She could well enjoy a rip-roaring sex life that puts yours in the shade. Erotic stories aimed at women work for some. If these graphic encounters feel a little too upfront (be prepared for extravagant descriptions of the act of sex), opt for the classics. D.H. Lawrence, Anaïs Nin or Erica Jong are all acceptable reading for the journey home from work. Keep an open mind about pornography. It's down to personal taste: porn films and magazines certainly do the trick for some women, while leaving plenty of others resolutely unimpressed. But resist the urge to compare yourself unfavourably with the silicone-enhanced actresses. Feeling inadequate or insecure about your body is not a promising beginning to a sexual encounter. Remember: any man will be deeply grateful to have a Sex Kitten in bed with him ...

2. Keep thinking sexy thoughts. Our society is so overloaded with sexual imagery in advertising, TV and movies that some women respond by shutting down sexual thoughts altogether. Remind yourself about sex a couple of times a day. Feeling stressed in the office? Imagine making love with that good-looking guy from marketing on your desk after work. Stuck at home with children who seem intent on creating Armageddon? Drift off into a fantasy about the tanned and toned window cleaner who just happened to turn up as you were emerging naked and wet from the shower ... The joy of a fantasy is that you don't have to be responsible, sensible or practise safe sex. It exists only in your mind and you can give yourself permission to do all kinds of things that you may never dare or even want to do in real life. Countless women fantasize about being treated roughly during sex by a powerful man who is overcome with lust at the sight of them. This certainly doesn't mean they'd like that experience in reality. Let your mind be a pleasure ground where you can fulfil every aspect of your sexual self. If you need inspiration, flick through the pages of Nancy Friday's enduring bestseller *My Secret Garden* for no-holds-barred descriptions of other women's sexual fantasies.

3. Imagine your ideal sexual encounter. Who are you with? Is it your partner, a movie star or the guy you exchanged a smile with on the way to work this morning? Where are you? Stretched out on white sand with the sun warming your skin or lying in front of a log fire in a cottage hideaway? What are you wearing? A smart business suit with devastatingly sexy lingerie underneath or a skimpy bikini? How passionate are you? Shy and demure or do you take charge and tease your lover into a frenzy of desire? Explore this fantasy to its fullest, and play it over in your mind at least three times a week.

4. Focus on aspects of your partner's body or behaviour that you find attractive. It's easy for the one you love to become a presence rather than a separate person when you have known him for a while. You forget to notice his sexy hands, his firm bum, his long, dark eyelashes, or any of the other physical attributes that once instantly sparked your desire to feel him inside you. And you take for granted aspects of his personality that you used to find exciting and different. If he still makes you laugh, openly appreciate it. If he's kind to children and animals, and that gives you a warm inner glow, let him know. Most women are turned on far more by personality and behaviour than by the passive male form. (Which is why men in uniforms are popular with lots of women. It's not the brass buttons, but the implication that these are go-getting guys who are brave, focused and think of others. Horny and hunky male firefighters are the focus of many a female sexual fantasy.) Reviewing what you like about your partner, *and* letting him know, serves as a double whammy. He gets to feel good about himself (and every man in the universe thrives on praise), and you get to be reminded of why you found him sexy in the first place.

5. Combat negative thoughts about sex. Past experiences may have given you the message that sex is best avoided. Such ideas need to be roundly challenged or they will regularly trip you up. If you were brought up to think that 'nice girls don't [enjoy sex]', replace that thought with 'nice girls do'. After all, an orgasm keeps you healthy. It releases beta-endorphins, natural painkillers that alleviate anxiety and trigger the release of the human growth hormone that plays a role in reducing fatty tissues and increasing lean muscles in various parts of the body. So sex relaxes you *and* makes you look younger! And let's face it, it's a cheaper and much more enjoyable alternative to Botox or expensive anti-wrinkle creams.

♥ *It's your call*

Many women think of sex as something that is somehow 'outside' themselves and their everyday experience. Even more see sex as something that is 'done' to them by a man, believing that responsibility for their pleasure or disappointment is definitely down to him. Some search for a lover who will magically transport them to a distant land of endless orgasm; others stick to one man but moan about him to their girlfriends, complaining that he's no good in bed and they'd choose chocolate or a cream cake over sex any day.

The truth is that far too many women abdicate responsibility for their own sexual pleasure. This isn't entirely surprising, but it is sad and ultimately damaging to relationships. So why do we do it? Well, it's partly down to the messages that we get from advertising, movies, music and magazines. These are incredibly powerful, and they reinforce a very narrow view of the sex act. This can be summarized as: woman (seductive) + man (overcome with lust) = a lot of pumping and gasping before both reach orgasm at exactly the same time.

As one perspective on sex, this is absolutely fine. As the sole role model for sexual encounters, it has been short-changing entire generations. It may suit some men and women some of the time, but it sure doesn't suit all of us all of the time. Imagine eating the same meal

My guess is that if you
go out to dinner or to a club,
you don't expect him
to order food or drinks
on your behalf . . . so why
should it be different
when it comes to sex?

every day; pretty soon you'd be fed up with it. If you constantly repeat the same pattern sexually, sooner or later you get very bored indeed. This isn't an argument for putting variety into your sex life, though that's important too. It's a way of explaining that it matters what both of you bring to the party, and that the two of you are equally responsible for your pleasure.

So, if you feel bored with your sex life, and you are tempted to blame your partner for being a disappointment, ask yourself 'How much information have I given this man about what I like?' My guess is that if you go out to dinner or to a club, you don't expect him to order food or drinks on your behalf. In fact, you might be irritated or even downright annoyed if he acted as though he knew what was best for you, without asking your preferences. So why should it be different when it comes to sex?

Men are not mind readers. They can't be expected to give you pleasure if you don't supply them with a map – or at least a few helpful directions. Far too many women put themselves out to learn how to please their man, but fail to offer him any information that he might find useful when it comes to pleasing them.

♥ *Exploring your inner sexiness*

A Sex Kitten understands the close link between sensuality and sexuality. She knows how to keep in touch with her needs and desires. By consciously and actively exploring her sensuality, she makes and maintains that vital connection with her sexual self.

You can begin that journey by opening yourself to simple, sensuous experiences because sometimes the brain *will* follow the body. If your body starts to tune in to something physically pleasurable, sexual thoughts begin to wake up too. For example, experiencing a soft wind on your skin is mildly arousing. That's why commercial photographers often use wind machines on photo shoots – advertisers want to give us the subliminal message that their product will make us feel good. (And remember that famous image of Marilyn Monroe in *The Seven Year Itch*, standing over the air vent, clutching her billowing skirt and squealing with delight?) Next time you go for a walk, decide to experience the breeze on your skin or even the raindrops on your face. All too often, we shut down sensations that we decide won't be pleasant, but open yourself to a range of physical feelings and you are helping to tune up your body's sexual response.

Cherish yourself, indulging all five senses. If you normally hurry through a three-minute shower in the morning, take things at a more leisurely pace one evening a week. Give up half an hour of TV to invest time in your body instead. Slowly massage fabulous-smelling lotion into your body after a bath or a shower, caressing your skin as if it were a lover's. Most of us touch ourselves in a way we would hate to be touched by another – we rush, we're slightly rough, and our minds are elsewhere. So gently, lovingly, get to know your body's curves and slopes, its dips and hollows.

Listen to music that makes you feel calm and energized at the end of a tiring day, experimenting to suit your mood. Eat food that tastes delicious, savouring every mouthful, rather than just shovelling in anything that fills you up. (You may lose weight too this way – more about that in the next chapter.)

Once you begin to realize that sensuality is a natural, spontaneous part of you, the next step is to accept that your sexuality works in exactly the same way. Try the two 'exercises' that follow. Each should be done when you are entirely alone – and on separate occasions. Prepare by setting aside some special time for yourself, just as if you were meeting a lover. This may feel slightly strange at first. Plenty of women feel more comfortable focusing on pleasing other people rather than themselves. But giving yourself some 'me-time' actually improves the quality of your relationships with others.

Open yourself to a range
of physical feelings
and you are helping to
tune up your body's
sexual response.

FOCUSING ON YOUR BODY

This one brings some surprisingly powerful results. Practised by people interested in Tantric sex, it involves moving sexual energy around your body. That may sound a little wacky, but the principles are similar to those of yoga. (And you don't have to be married to Sting or have children named Forest or Sky to benefit from it.) All you have to do is bounce your pelvis up and down for as long as you feel comfortable. It won't give you an orgasm in the conventional sense, but it is a great way to begin discovering some of the different sensations that your body can give you.

1. Lie comfortably on your back on your bed with your arms by your sides, palms facing upwards.

2. Bend your knees and keep your feet flat, hips' width apart.

3. Relax your neck and shoulders so that your neck is as straight and flat as is comfortable while keeping your jaw relaxed.

4. With your neck and shoulders still relaxed, raise your pelvis.

5. Begin to bounce your pelvis up and down, either rhythmically or experimenting with different speeds. (Sometimes playing music with a strong beat helps.) It may feel strange at first, but after a short while it should become easier. Do it for as long as feels comfortable.

6. When you stop, you may find that your body shakes or quivers as the energy travels upwards. (If you enjoy visualization, imagine a silver or golden light travelling to the top of your head and then tracing a line down the front of your body to settle in your navel.) Relax and enjoy the sensations you have stirred.

TAPPING INTO YOUR SEXUAL ENERGY

If you've never tried masturbating, or had a go and gave up because it didn't seem to work (some women say it's 'like tickling themselves'), don't be tempted to skip this experience. Learning how your own body works is essential information for building a good sexual relationship with another person. And if you already masturbate regularly, use this time to appreciate that self-pleasuring can be a whole-body experience that gives a major boost to your feel-good factor.

For this one you need to stock up on body lotion or massage oil and a water-based product such as KY lubricant (see page 126). Both will enhance sensation and that means more pleasure. Then, before you begin, create a warm and pleasing space, tidying away anything you would hide if you were expecting a guest.

1. Using body lotion or massage oil so that your hands glide easily across your skin, begin touching yourself as if for the first time. Stroke every other part of your body apart from your genitals. And if you have never masturbated before, relax!

2. With a water-based lubricant on your fingertips, rub your clitoris in small circles, keeping a steady rhythm. You'll know if you have applied too much lubricant because you'll feel less rather than more – you need a degree of friction if you are to experience an orgasm. The aim is to become familiar with the pace and touch that brings *you* the most pleasure. Some find touching their nipples at the same time is even more arousing; some find the tip of their clitoris almost too sensitive to be touched; and some find maximum pleasure by stimulating a wider area of their genitals. It may take between fifteen and thirty minutes (sometimes even longer) before you reach orgasm. Tipping your head backwards over the side of the bed may help bring you to climax faster, but don't do this if you have neck problems.

3. As you begin to give yourself pleasure, breathe as deeply and slowly as you can. Most people are inclined to tense up, but this actually reduces the sensations. Place your other hand on your heart: you may feel a warm tingling beneath your palm.

4. Try concentrating on your body and the feelings it is giving you. For many people, masturbation tends to be about releasing sexual tension, rather than enjoying the experience, and some people fear they won't be turned on without a fantasy playing in their heads. But you can be aroused simply by the sensations your body gives you and that's what you are exploring now.

5. Continue to breathe deeply when you reach orgasm. This actually intensifies the waves of exquisite pleasure and makes them last.

6. Don't leap up and get on with life straightaway afterwards. Cover yourself to stay warm, and lie quietly for a while, gently relaxing in the peaceful afterglow that washes over you.

Once you have the knack of connecting with your sexual energy, you may discover that all your physical and emotional sensations are heightened in exactly the same way as when you are first in love. Only this time these feelings aren't dependent on another person. They come from deep inside you, and it is up to you whether you share them with anyone else. It's a revelation to a lot of women that you don't need a partner to feel sexy. But one of the principal joys of being able to access your own sexual energy is that you will find that you are more in love with life itself.

Once you have the
knack of connecting
with your sexual energy,
you may discover that all
your physical and
emotional sensations
are heightened in exactly
the same way as when
you are first in love.

Self-esteem & self-image

Feline fine

Who do you think you are? Are you happy with yourself on the inside and the outside? Frequently the way women feel about sex is directly linked to the way they feel about their bodies and their emotions. The good news is that this can work both ways. Enjoying great sex with a lover can boost your self-esteem and make you feel better about your image. Equally, improving your self-esteem and self-image can dramatically boost your love life. Here's how ...

Naturally, a Sex Kitten has a good level of self-esteem – but what does this really mean? The term 'self-esteem' has become a label for describing the way you feel about yourself. And it matters because the way you feel about yourself governs practically every aspect of your behaviour, from the way you handle the guy you fancy to the way you decorate your bedroom.

Do you feel your boss listens to you and treats you with the respect you deserve? If you do, the chances are that your reasonably high level of self-esteem transmits itself to other people. And as a result they are more likely to treat you as an equal, at the very least. But if you feel you are one of those people who is walked over so often you might as well have 'Doormat' printed on the back of your T-shirt, it is likely that your self-esteem is fairly low. (And now is the time to start imagining that your T-shirt reads 'Superstar Sex Kitten' instead!)

♥ *Developing a positive view of yourself*

Sex Kittens know that self-esteem is a big factor in sexual attraction. If you like yourself and the way you look, you unconsciously send out messages to other people that give them permission to feel the same way about you. If, on the other hand, you feel uncomfortable with your body, and you are not proud of any of your achievements, you may have a hard time finding someone who wants to hang around long enough to convince you otherwise. Confidence is a magnet that draws other people towards you; low self-esteem usually sends them scurrying in the opposite direction.

So, before you sign up for striptease classes or a how-to-flirt course, examine your feelings, and if you are awash with negative beliefs about yourself, begin by considering how you might develop a more positive view. (A how-to-flirt course could be a good way of boosting your interaction with other people, by the way, but you will get more out of it if you see it as a sign of a change in your thinking, rather than using it simply as a sticking plaster to cover up a serious lack of self-belief.)

One crucial point here – it's no good having a high level of self-esteem if you don't have the skills to back it up. For example, it's pointless telling yourself that you'd make a great pop star if your pets or housemates always seem to make for the nearest exit whenever you open your mouth to sing. That's called self-delusion and it's no help at all when it comes to handling your life effectively.

So, true self-esteem follows, not precedes, the knowledge that you are performing well at any moment. You can't buy self-esteem with designer-label clothes, expensive handbags or that fantastic pair of stilettos you've just spotted in a shop window. (Sorry about that: many of us have tried at one time or another – and we've all found out that it doesn't work.) Sex Kittens know that retail therapy is effective only when it's fun, life enhancing and you can afford it. A wardrobe stuffed with guilt-inducing purchases, an empty feeling inside and an overdraft are not recommended. And lastly – but very importantly – self-esteem is never achieved or exercised at the expense of anyone else. Putting other people down won't convince anyone, least of all yourself, that you're worth it. Self-esteem comes from within and means …

Knocking negative self-criticism on the head This is one of the Sex Kitten's most useful techniques. Far too many women struggle with rigid ideas about how they need to act or look in order to be sexy and attractive, and so judge themselves lacking.

It only takes one negative thought like 'I'm too fat/old/grey-haired to be sexy' and a whole raft of negative behaviour is set in motion to back this up. You'll choose tent-like and dowdy clothes you think are appropriate for someone who is 'fat' or 'old'. You'll avoid buying anything you think is sexy because you've ruled 'sexy' isn't one of the adjectives that applies to you. Your behaviour will fit the model you

You don't have to drop
two dress sizes
or eradicate cellulite
to begin to feel great
about being you.

have of yourself and you won't feel right straying from this narrow vision of who you are. And you will miss out on the sensuous pleasure of dressing your body – and all the fun associated with it.

BUT if you can begin to counter these negative beliefs you will find your view of yourself embracing a much wider and more interesting definition of you. Just the thought 'I shall be sexy until I'm ninety' will make you smile and your *joie de vivre* will soar.

Feeling great in your own skin Do you look in the mirror and feel fine about the reflection that stares back at you? Or do you wince and look away? Or maybe you avoid mirrors altogether? Part of this chapter will offer the Sex Kitten's perspective on feeling good about your body, whatever your size or age. It is perfectly possible to change your body image without actually changing an inch of your body itself. In other words, you don't have to drop two dress sizes or eradicate cellulite to begin to feel great about being you.

Believing you can cope (and having a realistic understanding of your skills and abilities). This means that you don't need other people to prop you up emotionally or mentally. You don't have to take the weight of the world on your shoulders and single-handedly find a cure for starvation and poverty, but within your own world you *do* know how to handle certain situations and when you need to get help or support. You can rely on yourself in the tough times as well relishing the fun and frivolous moments.

This sounds extraordinarily simple, but it is remarkable how many people find it difficult. They drag themselves along from day to day, trying to keep their heads above water as they are washed backwards and forwards by wave after wave of disappointment. Possessing a reasonable level of self-esteem means that you have the inner resources to manage your life well, and also to make the most of opportunities that come your way.

SIX TIPS FOR BOOSTING LOW SELF-ESTEEM

If your self-esteem has always been low, or if it's taken a bashing recently after a relationship breakdown or a job disappointment, try these ways to turn things around.

1. Focus on six good things about your character. What do your friends like about you? Imagine you were your boss: how would you praise yourself?

2. Draw a mental picture of a positive, confident you. How will you behave, what will you be doing and what will the differences be between you now and in the future? Take time to think this through every night before you go to sleep.

3. Don't downgrade your achievements or minimize your successes; reflect on them and on the positive impact they have had on your life. A university degree may not have got you the job of your dreams, but very likely it gave you a set of friends for life. Perhaps you spotted a man whom instinct told you was trouble and you rooted him out of your life before he created havoc. Or perhaps you lived with a havoc-maker for a time and had the strength to walk away, even though it wasn't easy.

4. Check yourself each time you think negatively about an aspect of your personality that you assume is set in stone. It isn't. We are capable of making small and great changes in our lives. But if changing something major is too daunting, make small changes at first.

5. If low self-esteem means that you don't bother to look after yourself, start giving yourself one deliciously enjoyable treat a day. This shouldn't be something you feel you ought to do, or something you will feel guilty about afterwards. Make it something that will just brighten your day, like meeting a friend for coffee, buying a bunch of flowers for your desk, or listening to a favourite piece of music for as long as you like. Once this is working well, increase it to two treats a day – or more.

6. Practise the 'fake it till you make it' technique. Pull your tummy in, your shoulders back and walk tall. The higher our self-esteem, the higher we hold ourselves. It is possible to change feelings by working from the outside inwards. And just by carrying yourself differently, you can gain more confidence.

❤ *What is irresistible?*

Coco Chanel once said 'You can be gorgeous at twenty, charming at forty and irresistible for the rest of your life.' And she was right. A Sex Kitten understands that the myth of the skinny, twenty-year-old blonde with big boobs holds a powerful sexual sway over some men, but for the majority it is just that – a myth. For every man who fancies Beyoncé, there will be one who lusts after Judi Dench (and plenty of men have no difficulty fancying both). And there are even more men whose heart skips a beat when their own partner smiles sexily at them. Research has shown that men find their partners increasingly attractive the longer they are together.

If you don't believe this, listen to four men of different ages musing on what is sexy and what isn't …

SEXY A woman who is confident, relaxed and enjoys flirting.
NOT SEXY Someone who is uptight, serious and has no interest in her personal appearance.

Becoming a Sex Kitten
is not only a cheaper
alternative than cosmetic
surgery . . . it is a much
more effective route to
discovering your own
knockout sex appeal.

SEXY A woman who moves with sexual awareness. It's a look, a touch and knowing she is thinking sexy thoughts.
NOT SEXY Leggings. Huge silicone implants and a collagen pout. Poor hygiene.

SEXY Open and warm.
NOT SEXY Closed and cold.

SEXY Intelligence and black boots.
NOT SEXY Bad teeth and nagging.

Did you notice that not one of these men listed cosmetic surgery as sexy? In fact, one rated it definitely not sexy. Becoming a Sex Kitten is not only a cheaper alternative than cosmetic surgery (should you be considering it), it is a much more effective route to discovering your own knockout sex appeal.

If your response is that you look nothing like the women in porn magazines – because those women are meant to be sexy, aren't they? – and you fear that you won't measure up in the eyes of your partner, it's time to reassure yourself by thinking the whole thing through.

Pornography is about fantasy and control. Only the most insecure man would choose to masturbate over an image rather than make love to a real, live woman. Forget macho shows of bravado in front of his friends; never underestimate just how grateful the average man will be that you want to have sex with him in the first place.

If you have serious doubts about whether your partner really does like your body, just ask yourself two simple questions. Question Number One: have you ever relaxed enough to give him a proper chance to get to know it? Or are you usually too busy questioning him about the faults that you perceive? (Do I look fat today? And so on, and so on.) In other words, have you been projecting your insecurities and worries about your body onto him?

And Question Number Two: have you really listened when he has appreciated your body, or do you dismiss his remarks without thinking? Some women play destructive mind games with themselves when it comes to accepting compliments about the way they look. They have so conditioned themselves to dislike their bodies that hearing anyone say anything positive about them immediately produces a 'They can't possibly mean that' response. If you have squashed your partner's appreciation of your body on more than one occasion, don't be surprised if he gives up trying to get his message across.

If he is one of the rare men who are openly critical of their partner's body and makes disparaging remarks about your shape or size, think hard about your relationship. Some men, through insecurities of their own, try to demolish their partner's confidence in order to make them less attractive to other men. In effect, they are acting from a fear of losing their partner. But while you may be tempted to feel some sympathy, don't put up with it. A partner with this habit is troubled and needs help to understand that it is not a good way to keep a relationship going. You need to point this out, and watch for a change in behaviour, or make a speedy exit. A partner who cannot be trusted to admire and appreciate you physically is likely to be unreliable in other ways too. And any Sex Kitten can do better than this.

❤ *Do you yearn to look different?*

Do you hate your skinny arms/big nose/knobbly knees? Would you like to look like Cameron Diaz or Catherine Zeta Jones? Are you addicted to features in women's magazines that tell you how to dress and do your makeup like certain celebrities? If you are marooned on the island of 'if only I looked like', there's some good news and some bad news.

We'll start with the bad news. You are never going to look like someone else, so you might as well give up now. At best you'll appear a

If you are marooned
on the island of
'if only I looked like',
there's some good news
and some bad news.

pale imitation, and at worst you'll look like a bad impersonator. Try makeup and clothes tips from magazines by all means, but only if they help you develop your own style rather than adopt a faint echo of someone else's. Now, the good news: you can become so comfortable in your own skin, whatever your age, shape or size, that striving to look like someone else seems a sad waste of time. Why should you try to be another woman when you can have far more fun being fabulous, confident, sexy you?

How do you do it? Firstly, remember the Sex Kitten's approach to 'body imperfections'. *The chances are you are far more aware of them than anybody else.* It is even possible that something that you consider a hideous fault is deemed desirable by someone else. For every big-busted woman who gets fed up lugging her 38DD bosom around, there is a small-breasted one looking enviously on who is harbouring thoughts of breast implants. For years I despaired of my skinny, narrow feet. Then came the day when I was standing barefoot and another woman admired my 'elegant toes'. When I'd worked out that she wasn't having a laugh at my expense, I decided to 'reframe' my view of my feet. There are still shoes so wide I can fit both feet inside just one of the pair, but over the years I have tracked down some reasonably desirable narrow ones as well. And, thanks to that one remark from a relative stranger, I don't hate my feet any more.

If worrying about your weight is your problem and you are caught in an endless cycle of dieting and guilt about food, accept that, as with improving any kind of low self-esteem, you will have to retrain your thinking. Stop comparing yourself to other women and begin by considering these three facts.

Sex Kittens pity fashion models Most models have eating disorders and are up to 19 per cent below the recommended weight for their height. (One of the main diagnostic criteria for the life-limiting illness anorexia nervosa is being more than 16 per cent below your recommended weight.) So, instead of skimming through the fashion pages enviously, try reframing your attitude to those pictures. Feel pity for women who are depriving themselves of the pleasure of food so they can maintain a dangerously low weight.

Sex Kittens know body shape is neutral Fatness and thinness are matters of fashion. One of life's ironies is that as we grow bigger Western society has decreed that slimness is a virtue, and as a result millions of women go on pointless weight-loss diets that make them grumpy and miserable. Restricting your food intake is depressing and, as you will know if you have opted to try more than one diet, rarely a permanent solution to losing weight.

Sex Kittens are kind to their bodies Punishing your body by starving it, or by bingeing on junk food, is not the way to get the best out of it. Good food nourishes your body and your spirit. Food should be a source of pleasure, not guilt and despair. Redressing the balance between your mind and your body in relation to food is crucial if you are to embrace your body and the joys it can bring you.

Some time ago, I was particularly struck by a remark by Natalie Kusz in her essay 'The Fat Lady Sings', included in the US bestseller *The Bitch in the House*. She describes how, after years of useless dieting, abuse from passing strangers, and lectures from doctors, she decided to 'suspend body-related thought' and just live her life. She acknowledges that hers is not an ideal role-model, but she has chosen to step outside the Western obsession with weight and size.

> It's not that the naysayers don't have a point. I will die young. I will, perhaps, suffer diseases like diabetes, arteriosclerosis, and joint deterioration. But I will have written books. I will have parented well. I will have taken care of an ailing father and survived his death, as well

41

as the death – young, herself – of my mother. My headstone will not read, "She never let herself go," but neither will it say, "She was as big as a barge." It will, I hope, say something like "She knew Truth and Substance and abided in them."

Natalie Kusz is a big woman in every sense of the word: physically, mentally and spiritually. You may not want to replicate her stance on size (and for health reasons that probably wouldn't be a good idea), but her attitude towards her life is admirable. She has nailed the idea that women have to obsess about their weight by choosing to focus on things that are inherently far more worthwhile.

If you are constantly dieting, just pause for a moment and imagine what you could achieve if you put all that mental energy into a different project. You could write a book, climb a mountain, take up water-skiing or just enjoy the things you are currently doing so much more. Try the exercise outlined below if you want to get off the dieting treadmill.

THE DIET-FREE WAY TO YOUR IDEAL SHAPE

Achieving and maintaining the ideal weight and shape for your genetic makeup is less a matter of avoiding certain foods, and more about identifying and re-connecting with the natural signals your body sends your awareness to keep you at the optimum level of health and wellbeing. This means retraining yourself to eat slowly. (And thinking about how food feels when it reaches your stomach rather than your mouth.) To speed up the process, include a little exercise in your daily routine (no less than twenty minutes of medium-to-brisk walking).

1. Throw away your scales and resolve to measure your progress by your own signals. This means that you'll notice the way your clothes fit better, how your body feels and looks in the mirror, and your sense of increased wellbeing.

2. You are setting up a new relationship with food so don't eat until you are really hungry. Notice what real hunger feels like.

3. Then, and only then, decide what you would like to eat. Turn off the TV or radio, put aside anything you might be tempted to read, and prepare that particular food.

4. Always sit down at a table to eat.

5. Eat slowly, using your senses to savour the food. Be aware of how it looks, smells, tastes, its texture … even the way it sounds as you chew.

6. After you swallow each mouthful, attend to its progress downwards until you are certain it has reached your stomach, and then decide whether you want any more. Then, and only then, repeat the process, eating each mouthful with full attention, and following it until it reaches your stomach.

7. Be aware of the point at which you feel pleasantly satisfied, and stop, even if it means leaving food on your plate.

8. Notice how much you enjoy your food when you eat this way, and how easy it is to stop well before you feel bloated. There is no sense of deprivation because you will have eaten food you like, enjoyed it thoroughly and known throughout that you are free to eat whatever you are drawn to … as long as you are hungry when you do so.

To imprint these steps on your unconscious mind and your physical responses, follow this programme for between fourteen and twenty-one consecutive meals. After that, eat whenever it feels right, noticing what you want, and checking from time to time through the meal how near you are to that pleasant feeling of satisfaction.

♥ *Feeling good about your size*

The most important fact to remember is *self-image has nothing to do with the way you actually look.* This is not as strange as it might sound. Think about it. You could be a tall, skinny blonde model, get turned down for work by a photographer who looks at you, frowns and shakes his head, and feel you are the most unattractive creature on the planet. And for women who do conform to the media's current template of what's desirable, there is the added uncertainty of whether you are wanted for you, or just because your looks are popular with certain kinds of men. Alternatively, you might be distinctly average-looking, compared with the women in celebrity magazines, but feel fine about yourself and have men falling at your feet. Simply by accepting yourself as you are, you are sending signals to other people to do the same.

A survey by Britain's *Good Housekeeping* magazine saw curvaceous actress Dawn French voted top role-model by a thousand teenage girls. Writing in *The Times*, columnist Jonathan Gornall commented:

> Every woman I have known would aspire to being as funny and confident as Dawn French, but few would go out of their way to pile on her pounds. Whatever they say in surveys, weight – or, at least, shape – is more important to most women than almost anything … The irony is that men expect a lot less of women than women demand of themselves (and of other women). Essentially – and women would revolutionise their social lives if only they trusted in this – there is little sexier for a man than a woman who is comfortable in her own skin: that confidence counterbalances extra pounds and inches in a way that sexy underwear and too much make-up never can.

He went on to say that men are in a no-win situation when they try pointing this out to any woman, and illustrated this with poet John Hegley's summary of the dilemma:

I said Pat

you are fat

and you are cataclysmically desirable

and to think I used to think

that slim was where it's at

well not any more Pat

you've changed that

and love yourself

and flatter yourself

and shatter their narrow image of the erotic

and Pat said

what do you mean FAT?

Sounds familiar? Remember the lists of what men find sexy? No one mentioned not liking big thighs, cellulite or wrinkles, yet many women spend a small fortune on gym membership and face creams just trying to eliminate them.

It is great to go to a gym to keep yourself fit, and it's fine to use face cream if it gives you a boost. But every Sex Kitten knows the following fact of life. *Given a choice between a woman who tries to keep her thighs hidden and doesn't kiss her man for fear of wiping off her expensive face cream, and a woman who hops into bed looking enthusiastic and pleased to be with him, there's no contest.* Enthusiasm beats physical perfection ninety-nine times out of a hundred. And if you are stuck with the one bloke in a hundred who rates physical perfection above all else, you might want to consider finding another man. Believe me, you will certainly have much more fun elsewhere.

Accept your body as it is now. Don't put off dressing in sexy clothes until you have gone down a dress size, got a tan or toned up your arm muscles. You still have the option of changing yourself in future if it really matters to you, but at least you won't be postponing forever the day when you can enjoy being who you are.

If changing how you feel about your whole body feels like too great a leap, decide on just one aspect of your body that you feel OK with. Do you like your hair/bosom/legs/feet? Now focus on it. Treat yourself to a regular professional blowdry so your hair always looks great; buy a low-cut top that shows off your décolletage; wear sexy shorts in the summer; invest in some strappy sandals. Enjoy that one aspect of your body and then, as your confidence grows, focus on other areas too.

♥ *There is no cut-off point to being sexy*

It isn't only society's attitude to body shape that makes women uncertain of their own attractiveness. Age is another issue the media drag up to berate women. Certain newspapers revel in printing close-ups of famous female faces as they get older, implying that to grow older is to exceed the sell-by date of your sex appeal.

But Sex Kittens know there is no cut-off point to being sexy. OK, when you are eighty you may find you have most success with your contemporaries, but don't be surprised if you stay a man-magnet forever. This is because being a Sex Kitten is about contacting the good feelings inside you and sharing them with other people. The result: a charisma that only increases the longer you develop it. And yes, this works a treat for your sex life, but you will find that changing the way you think about yourself boosts all your relationships.

♥ *Clothes*

So you think Sex Kittens wear fluffy mules, silk stockings, slinky negligées and not much else? They do – but only sometimes. Sex Kittens are everywhere, leading lives as lawyers, teachers, doctors, nurses, stay-at-home mums, nuclear scientists … And, of course, they aren't doing those things in their scanties. But they *are* dressed in ways that make them feel confident and good about themselves.

Taking an interest in what you wear doesn't make you shallow or vain. Clothes give out vital messages about you. Losing all interest in what you wear is actually a sign of clinical depression. The costume historian James Laver wrote in *Costume and Style*: '[Clothes] are nothing less than the furniture of the mind made visible.'

So think about your wardrobe for a moment. What do the clothes hanging in there say about the furniture of *your* mind? Do they demonstrate that you like your body and feel good about yourself? Or do you use clothes to cover up a body you are dissatisfied with? Are they a reflection of the feeling that somehow you don't measure up? Are the clothes you choose not a celebration of the person you are, but more a way of hiding your unhappiness with yourself?

We all find it easy to be overwhelmed by negative feelings about ourselves, but remember that positive actions can change feelings. So you don't necessarily have to start feeling better about your body before you begin to get rid of the 'just-cover-me-up' clothes in your wardrobe.

When you are next window-shopping and you see something you like, say a bright colour, but find yourself automatically dismissing it from your mind in favour of your usual neutral shade or black, stop for a moment and ask yourself 'Why am I making this choice?' If the answer is that you are opting for a cover-up rather than a 'this makes me feel great' item of clothing, either buy what you were first drawn to or don't buy anything at all.

Your first step may be just to stop adding to the clothes that don't make you feel good. As you become more aware of your habits and the negative voice inside your head ('That would be OK if I lost a stone', and so on), begin to challenge them. The next step is to buy something that inspires you and determine to wear it immediately.

♥ *Look like a Sex Kitten in 30 minutes*

Transforming yourself on the inside may take a little longer

Five minutes Jump into the shower, but don't spend ages covering yourself in perfume and body lotion afterwards. If you do, you'll simply mask the smell of your pheromones, which are the scent version of a fingerprint. Our olfactory organs can sense less than one hundred-millionth of a gram of musk and the impact on the brain is immediate. Smell affects our emotional reactions more than any other sense, and your pheromones, released from apocrine glands, found in the armpits, groin, mouth, nipples, backs of the knees, wrists and palms, play an important role in attracting your partner to you.

Ten minutes (optional) Wash and dry your hair, but don't feel you have to spend ages styling it to perfection. In fact, the slightly messy 'just got out of bed' look is popular with most men, probably because they like to imagine they've been in bed with you, having a wild time; however, this applies only to shiny, clean hair. Don't rely on the wild look if it needs a wash.

Two minutes Put on some lipstick and, if you really want to make an impact, add a trace of lip gloss too. It's not something we talk about (or even consciously think about), but makeup is designed to attract a partner by mimicking the sexual organs. Colouring our lips red sends a non-verbal signal of sexual arousal (the lips outside the vagina plump up and redden just before orgasm), and lubrication in the area increases when we are aroused (hence the lip gloss). Watch for it and you will find that you lick your lips whenever you come up against someone or something you find arousing.

Five minutes A touch of mascara and eyeliner will draw attention to your eyes. Our eyes are capable of responding to one and a half million simultaneous messages, and eye contact is one of the most critical ways in which you interact with other people. If you look at someone you find attractive, you tend to blink more frequently (hence the phrase 'fluttering your eyelashes'). Equally, the more you blink at someone, the more attracted to them you feel. And you make the other person blink more frequently too ... (see page 61). All of which explains the popularity of false eyelashes in certain eras.

One minute Brush your eyebrows into shape. They are important indicators of sexual interest too. When you first see someone you find attractive, your eyebrows rise and fall. If he finds you attractive, he reflects the gesture. It lasts about a fifth of a second and, for the most part, we do it completely unconsciously. According to sex expert Tracey Cox in her book *Superflirt:*

> Lifting the brows pulls the eyes open and allows more light to reflect off the surface, making them look bright, large and inviting. An eyebrow flash might be easy to miss but they're so reliable, if you do spot one, you may know someone fancies you before they've even registered it themselves. Deliberately extend it for up to one second and you've drastically upped the chances of him getting the message you're interested.

So don't get carried away and pluck your eyebrows into oblivion. They are a handy tool in the mating game.

Six minutes and 55 seconds Get dressed. You don't have to invest a fortune in expensive underwear, but do make sure that what you wear is matching, comfortable and makes you feel good. Pretty much the same applies to your outerwear too.

Forget 'Does my bum
look big in this?'
Celebrate if it does.
Bottoms are sexy.

Tactile fabrics, like fake fur and velvet, satin, silk and even very fine wool, don't just feel nice: they wake up your senses. (Sex Kittens understand, of course, that 'dressing up' isn't just about delighting their partner; it's about fine tuning their own sensations and creating more fun for themselves too.)

Five seconds Slip on a pair of high heels. And forget 'Does my bum look big in this?' Celebrate if it does. Bottoms are sexy. All the other female primates send sexual signals via the colour and smell of their bottoms, which as they walk on all fours is relatively easy for them. High heels lengthen your legs and make your bottom stick out by a further 25 per cent. This explains why, given a choice between seeing their partner in a pair of high heels or a pair of Doc Martens, the majority of men would opt for the heels every time.

You're on The secret of looking good for an entire evening is to make an effort before you go out and then forget what you look like. Remember the Sex Kitten's motto: *Focus on making the best of yourself first, and then focus on getting the best out of everyone around you.*

Body language

Twitching your tail or
licking your paws?

Gaining Sex Kitten status isn't just a matter of feeling good about yourself. It's also about understanding the impact that you have on other people, and being able to read the signals they are giving out. It's no use coming up with a sparkling bon mot *worthy of Oscar Wilde if your body language says you are a humourless depressive. And you need to be able to spot the signs when a potential mate is interested or you could be missing out on a lot of fun ...*

Research has shown that the actual words you use account for as little as *7 per cent of the overall impression you make on someone.* Your tone of voice, the clothes you wear, the way you move and stand, your gestures and physical responses account for the rest. You walk around giving out information about yourself the whole time. But most of us barely recognize this. If we do think about how we appear to other people, we tend to concentrate on the most superficial, external details. So we might get a new haircut to change our image, or buy a sexy outfit if we feel our sex appeal is on the slide.

While these actions have some effect, it will be pretty limited unless you accompany them with a shift in the body-language messages you are transmitting as well. What's the point of slipping on a cleavage-revealing silk shirt, only to sit with hunched shoulders, crossed arms and pursed lips? But change your body language to open and inviting, and you'll find that even muddy dungarees and a man's checked shirt can look sexy.

PLUS, if you are going to get really smart, being able to recognize a few body-language basics in other people gives you a head start in making successful relationships. Otherwise you might as well be operating in blinkers and earmuffs – you are just not receiving all the information available. Being aware of the signals you give out – and being able to read other people's signals – opens up a new lexicon of understanding between you and the rest of the world.

And when it comes to physical attraction, having a few body-language tricks up your silky sleeve will make connecting with potential partners a lot more fun for both of you. For example, you can turn around a so-so conversation with someone by doing nothing more dramatic than changing the way you stand and the way you listen. Simply angle your torso towards him, and maintain eye contact for 75 per cent of the time – when most people talk, they look at one another for only 30 to 60 per cent of the time. (There will be more on eye contact later in this chapter.)

💜 *The signals you give out*

Body language is part of the circle of human behaviour. You think, feel, act, think again and so on; it is a loop that governs the way we interact with other people. Your 'natural' body language has been acquired over your lifetime. Some of it you will have learnt from your parents and family. (Are you 'touchy feely', for example, or is your instinct to freeze when you are given an unexpected hug?) The rest is a combination of your current attitude to your body and your varying confidence levels in social situations.

Changing your body language so that it works for you, instead of against you, is a skill. The more you practise, the better you get. An unexpected bonus of building your body-language skills is that it can also change your feelings. This is because the brain takes in messages from your body as well as giving them out, and you may find that if you stand straighter and begin to act in a more confident way, sooner or later you will actually *feel more confident.* This isn't cheating; it is simply a different way of learning a skill, and one already described as the 'fake it till you make it' technique (see page 35).

Deliberately changing your body language in social situations is not a sign of a manipulative schemer. It makes sense to be in control of the way you interact with other people, especially if you intend to use the skill positively. After all, you edit the words you use in conversation. You are unlikely to greet someone with the words 'Great to see you – my, that's a big spot on the end of your nose!' Politeness or social conditioning will restrict you to the first exclamation, unless you don't mind making an enemy for life.

Well, a limp handshake can certainly undermine a warm greeting, and crossed arms and legs will always make you look defensive, no matter what you say. Monitoring your body language is the physical equivalent of editing your conversation: a way of keeping a closer rein on how other people perceive you.

A happy and
relaxed person who
looks as if she is
having a good time is
the biggest draw of all.

YOUR BODY-LANGUAGE STARTER KIT

These seven basic tips can all be used in social situations. Remember that an old habit can be changed in as little as twenty-one days and a new habit can be acquired much faster. Even so, if you are only just beginning to work on your body language, don't try every tip on the same evening. You may be so busy flirting with a wine glass and wiggling as you walk that you forget to enjoy yourself, and a happy and relaxed person who looks as if she is having a good time is the biggest draw of all.

1. Smile at appropriate moments with your lips apart and your mouth not too far open. Extend the smile to your eyes so they soften and crinkle. (Yes, a genuine smile makes your eyes wrinkle, which is why describing lines around your eyes as 'laughter lines' is more accurate and preferable to the ugly-sounding 'crow's feet').

2. Laugh – don't guffaw. An over-loud laugh is a sign of attention-seeking behaviour, and makes most of the people around you feel uncomfortable. If nature has blessed you with a slightly husky voice, however, you may find men fall at your feet. This is because our voices deepen slightly during sexual arousal, so a gravelly female voice suggests a woman who enjoys a roll in the hay. I don't recommend smoking twenty a day to get this effect, though. Your voice may well sound huskier, but potential suitors are likely to be put off by the smell of cigarettes clinging to your clothes – and the smoker's cough.

3. Occasionally – and I mean *occasionally* – stroke your hair or neck, and touch your mouth or the stem of your wine glass. These are sexual gestures as far as men are concerned so doing them frequently is overkill. And too much hair-stroking also makes you look vain and self-obsessed.

4. Don't tap your fingers or feet unless you are about to dance
It suggests aggression.

5. Appear energetic. There's no need to leap from barstool to barstool: just don't slump or hunch in a corner. Would-be partners respond to vitality and enthusiasm.

6. Wear high heels. I know I've mentioned them before, but they change the way you walk. In terms of attracting male attention, it's as successful as laying a trail of sweets on the carpet for a baby. And be aware of your pelvis as you walk. Marilyn Monroe said people often ignored her in the street until she put on 'The Walk'.

7. Don't gesticulate wildly while you talk, or finish what you say with a laugh (unless you are telling a funny story). Flapping hands and nervous laughter undermine what you are saying, making it look as if you have no confidence in your own opinions.

♥ *Using eye contact*

Poets talk about eyes being the windows of the soul for a very good reason. You can make intimate contact with another person using just your eyes. And when your eyes connect, your communication can shift to a deeper level. If you want to move your conversation onto an even more intimate footing in double-quick time, maintain eye contact during the silence after you have finished speaking. It can have a powerful effect.

The Harvard-based US social psychologist Zick Rubin produced the first scientific scale to measure how much affection couples feel for each other called, appropriately enough, Rubin's Scale. His study 'The Measurement of Romantic Love' offered official confirmation of two facts we all know – people who are deeply in love gaze at each other much more when they talk, and they are slower to look away when someone else enters their space. Often, if they do look away, they will turn back at the same time and continue to stare into each other's eyes, mirroring their partner's behaviour. (Other people around them subconsciously note what's going on and tend to leave the starry-eyed couple alone.)

As with all body-language matters, you need to use common sense when applying this knowledge, as too much eye contact can appear aggressive or threatening. Hold your companion's gaze for 75 per cent of the time and you may well trigger the cocktail of love chemicals that binds mutually attracted strangers to one another when they first meet. Lock eyes with him 100 per cent of the time and he may start nervously looking around for your minder.

To play the eye-contact game well, begin by drawing attention to your eyes. Tracey Cox in *Superflirt* recommends pushing your hair away from your eyes or tapping near them with a pen. She also suggests a quick trick with a double whammy: put your thumb underneath your chin and rest your first and second fingers on the side of your head. Not only does this draw attention to your eyes, but you are also pointing to your brain, giving out the subliminal message that you are intelligent too.

At some stage in your conversation, your eyes will need to travel away from your companion's eyes, and you may find that they begin to make a journey southwards, depending on just how sexually attractive you find him. With a stranger, you will probably look from eye to eye, and occasionally dip to the bridge of his nose. With a friend, on the other hand, your gaze will probably take in the whole of his nose and mouth. With a lover, your eyes may travel down to his genitals and back, though the chances are that you won't be consciously thinking along Mae West lines 'Is that a bicycle pump in his pocket or is he just pleased to see me?'

Try thinking
sexy, positive thoughts
about the person
you are talking to.

Dilated pupils are another sign of serious interest. Pupils widen when we see or think about something we like. It is an involuntary response: a signal from our unconscious to someone else's that we are interested. But if you aren't sure you can trust your unconscious to get the message across by itself – and you would like to be certain your eyes are working for you – you could try thinking sexy, positive thoughts about the person you are talking to. The chances are your pupils will immediately dilate and they will be conveying those messages faster than you think.

If you find that your lover's gaze is lingering longingly on your mouth before returning to your eyes, it is likely that he finds you very attractive. If, on the other hand, you become aware that you are in a relationship with a man whose eye contact is minimal and whose face remains impassive when he sees you, there's probably something fairly major that needs to be sorted (assuming he's not had Botox injections or an unsuccessful facelift). If you find someone closing his eyes while talking to you, it probably means he is seriously stressed and wants literally to shut out the world. Give up for the moment if you are hoping to spark his interest, and wait until he has sorted out whatever it is that is making him so exhausted.

And finally, while we are talking about eyes, a word here about the impact of the humble eye blink. Yes, a blink does a great job of washing debris off your eyeballs, but it also works at an entirely different level. Rapid blinking sends a message to the brain that we find someone attractive, and as a result the brain starts to fire off the love chemicals that whizz round our bodies when we first fall for someone. So, if you find a man attractive, you will automatically begin to blink faster, unless you are concentrating really hard on following every word he is saying, in which case the act of concentration will mean you blink less. Sorry, there are no hard-and-fast rules when it comes to body language.

If you want to make the person you are attracted to feel more attracted to you, deliberately blink more often and it is likely that he will unconsciously increase his blink rate to match yours. As a result, you will both feel more attracted to each other, although whether this will still be the case when you eventually give your eyelids a rest will remain to be seen …

♥ *Don't approach a man from the front*

If you have just made fleeting eye contact with a guy across the room and would like to get to know him better, be wary of walking up to face him. There's some wired-in prehistoric data here telling men that if they are about to be attacked it is usually by someone standing directly in front of them. But that doesn't mean you have to sneak up behind him and tap him on the shoulder. A sideways approach usually works well, and then you can ease yourself round to stand in front of him as the conversation begins. (Women are less comfortable with approaches from behind or even sideways on, which probably stems from their instinctive fear of being overpowered by unseen big, burly blokes.)

♥ *Watch those thumbs*

Before we move on to interpreting other people's body language, just one more point to bear in mind that you may not have come across before. Think about your thumbs. Tracey Cox points out that assertive people invariably have their thumbs sticking up or out on show. Confident women, she says, will often leave their thumbs out when they put their hands in their pockets. And men will fold their arms across their chest, fingers under their armpits (conveniently making their biceps look bigger) with both thumbs left out on their chest and pointing upwards. While the folded arms may seem protective, thumbs-up is actually a gesture of confidence. If a man is turning his torso

Be wary of walking up to
face a guy you fancy.
There's some wired-in
prehistoric data here telling
men that if they are about
to be attacked it is usually by
someone standing directly
in front of them.

towards you at the same time and making eye contact, it is likely that he is keen to get to know you better.

Six signals that show how interested he is

What should you look out for? These are the clues that tell you he is interested in you … (It takes a man thirty seconds to decide whether a woman is his type or not. A woman usually makes up her mind in three seconds. Go, girls.)

1. 'Chest-banging' displays – as psychologists call them – usually involve the need to show off in some way, whether it's flipping beer mats or driving fast. Generally, women find this kind of behaviour fairly tedious, and most men sense they need to get it over quickly if they are to succeed with you, but take note because it does indicate that he wants to impress.

2. He occasionally strokes his tie. This is drawing your attention downwards to his penis (entirely unconsciously, of course). If he constantly indulges in tie-stroking, however, it is a gesture of insecurity and self-comfort. Also beware if he strokes the tip of his nose – he may be lying. Hearts react to stress by pumping blood faster through the tiny surface capillaries, causing our noses to swell by a fraction of a millimetre. The result is sometimes a tiny tingling that people may respond to by touching.

3. A man will often widen his stance when he is standing in front of a woman he likes. This accentuates what body-language experts dub 'the crotch display'. If he is holding a drink, he will drop it to waist height, or perhaps even lower. And when he talks to you, he may bounce up and down on his toes, which has the effect of simulating pelvic thrusting during sex.

4. Watch where his hands move as you are talking. Men and women tend to touch themselves where they would like to be touched if they are talking to someone they find attractive. One word of warning though – if he covers his mouth it probably means he's not interested. The mouth plays a key role in sexual body-language so covering it is not encouraging. And pursing the lips is a real downer. It's a throwback to the days when bad food could kill you, so if your companion begins to wrinkle his mouth you are probably not onto a winner.

5. If a man crosses his legs while talking to you, he may not be finding you particularly attractive. If he lays one leg across the other, with the calf resting on the thigh and holds the top leg, his message is pretty much 'Leave me alone'.

6. Heard the expression 'Pull your socks up'? Well, that's exactly what men do if they are interested in a nearby female. It is a preening gesture that means he wants to look his best, as does smoothing (or mussing up) his hair (depending on his favoured style), fiddling with his shirt or jacket, and standing with his muscles flexed and his hands on his hips. His fingers will be pointing to his genitals, demonstrating his finest assets and showing where he would like to be touched …

Sex &
the Single
Kitten

Finding someone to stroke your fur?

You don't need a partner to be sexy and you don't have to feel desperate (or even mildly worried) if you don't have a partner. Contrary to popular belief, sexy feelings exist inside you all the time; they aren't limited to what happens between the sheets in the land of coupledom. Feeling sexy is about being in touch with all your senses, and experiencing the joy of being truly, wildly, excitingly alive ...

One of the biggest myths about couple relationships is that a partner makes us whole. There are two versions that pop up in stories from fairy tales to Shakespeare. One is the Cinderella fantasy. Generally, it features two lonely people who find each other and instantly all their problems are solved. So dowdy Cinders says 'goodbye' to material and emotional poverty, and 'hello' to great clothes, fabulous wealth and a loving prince. (This is very popular with little girls.) The other is the Romeo and Juliet complex. Two people find they cannot live without each other but their love has tragic consequences. Usually, one (or both) of them ends up dead. (This is very popular with operatic composers and TV soap writers.)

Both versions hinge on the belief that neither person can survive successfully without the other. Togetherness is everything. Love means no separation. Now, while this makes for great storytelling, applying the principle has disastrous results in real life. Either people lead empty lives, searching for someone who will make them complete, or those already in relationships hand over responsibility for their contentment to their partner, and eventually become disillusioned when he or she fails to deliver.

The fact that we are each responsible for our own happiness within our relationships is something not widely acknowledged. Sadly, some people lead their whole lives misunderstanding this fundamental truth of human existence. So, when the 'in love' stage with its overwhelming, feel-good hormones begins to fade, they start to experience a sense of let-down. Their partner doesn't appear to be making them feel great any more. It's the moment when many people decide that things just aren't working and give up. Sometimes they leave; sometimes they stay. If they hang on, the relationship usually shrivels slowly under the weight of mutual disappointment.

What these people don't understand is that the good feelings they think were ignited by someone else *actually existed inside themselves already*. Happiness is simply a question of learning to gain access to the good feelings inside you. Which is why being single can be as fulfilling an experience as being part of a couple. In some cases, even more so, because the good feelings you generate in yourself can't be quashed by a partner's woes. That's not to say that singletons live in a bubble, protected from the bad feelings of others. But they may have a much greater chance of maintaining their own equilibrium and managing their destinies unhindered by the problems and insecurities of someone else.

(And who's going to moan if you buy the same pair of shoes in three different colours, want to watch six episodes of *Sex and the City* back to back, or use up all the hot water for one huge, luxuriously scented foam bath?)

That point about not seeking happiness in someone else applies to our sexual energy too. For most of us, a new relationship sparks a sexual awakening; we feel sexier, we want to make love anywhere, everywhere; and there's a spring in our step and a wiggle in our hips. But we don't realize that the well of sexual energy that suddenly makes us feel so great was *inside us already*. ('Sexual energy', of course, is that pleasurable pulse of desire you have when you see someone you are attracted to, or the delightful frisson you experience as you read a sexy novel or watch a sexy movie.)

♥ *Sex Kittens can be successfully single*

Of course, good relationships are wonderfully rewarding and, for most of us, they are a major part of our lives. But they alone should not define how happy we are or how sexy we feel. Joyfulness and sexiness come from inside us. We can share them with another person; we can't expect another person to provide them for us. So let's be clear. This chapter is not about tracking down a mate who will make you happy. It is about attracting someone you can share your good feelings with – if

Wear fabulous
underwear
even if you are the
only person
who is going to see it.

you choose to do so. And, if you are a Sex Kitten flying solo at the moment, the most important thing to remember is that sexiness doesn't occur in response to another person – it starts inside you.

This isn't just about being responsible for your own sexual pleasure (see page 19 for more on that). It is about treating yourself with the love and respect you would give a partner. So how well do you care for yourself physically and emotionally? If you are better at looking after others than yourself, the chances are you don't engage very much with your inner sexiness.

Sexy people feel good because they look after themselves, as well as others. If this is a novel idea for you, make a few small changes and note the impact they have. Wear fabulous underwear even if you are the only person who is going to see it. Embark on some kind of experience that is purely about fun for you, whether that's joining a book club or learning to belly dance. (No prizes for guessing which might wake up your inner sexiness fastest.) And generally remember to treat yourself as the sexy, vibrant creature you truly are.

❤ *What if you don't want to be single?*

If you decide to share your sexiness with someone else, how do you find a partner to stroke your fur? Whole books are devoted to this subject, but most of them don't mention a few key relationship facts.

Fact 1 Your beliefs about yourself condition all your relationships. So it is worth examining them before you even begin to consider building a relationship with someone else. Not only will they affect whom you meet (think 'I'm hopeless with men' and straightaway you are limiting the likelihood of meeting a potential partner), they will also have a major impact on any couple relationship you make (think 'I'll be lucky to find a man who wants to marry me' and it's unlikely your marriage will be a respectful partnership of equals). Alternatively, believe that there are lots of guys out there you could strike up a great relationship with, and it's likely you'll soon be meeting more than your fair share. Consider yourself a prize worth fighting over, and you may not have two hunks tussling on the bar-room floor for your favours (that's so Jerry Springer, after all) but at the very least you will find yourself valued highly by your partner.

Fact 2 You don't have to go to singles bars, join a dating agency or take up car-maintenance evening classes in the hope of meeting eligible men. Take up hobbies that give you pleasure, by all means, but don't bother casting your eyes around ceaselessly to see who's out there.

Fact 3 Heavy-duty flirting with every male under eighty in the desperate hope that *someone* will ask you out is a time-waster. Flirting only works if it is about making a genuine connection with someone else. That means taking an honest interest in the other person, *and* making them feel good, rather than engaging in endless sexual banter or acting in an overly sexy way to draw attention to yourself.

A Sex Kitten has the knack of sharing her good feelings with other people, and making the object of her flirtation feel good about himself too. This winning combination of mental attitude and body language will work for you at any age, irrespective of your looks, income or job. Learn the art and you will never lack people who want to get to know you. Flirt like a Sex Kitten and you will probably find that there's always a host of willing suitors waiting for the green light wherever you are.

But remember, too, that you don't need a partner to make you happy. Acquire the knack of contentment as a solo Sex Kitten and you instantly multiply your choices in life. (You never have to stay in an unhappy relationship, for example, because you are scared by the thought of being on your own.)

♥ *And what if you do (want to be single)?*

If you are in a relationship and you think you might be happier as a single Sex Kitten, you may need to ask yourself some tough questions about your partner. And don't be afraid if your answers signal that you'd be better off without the relationship. Someone once said that 'Love is friendship set on fire' and even the most lust-fuelled love will fizzle out without a decent friendship at its base.

Generally speaking, you need about five positive experiences to every negative one for a relationship to be stable. If you realize that the bad times are outnumbering the good, or even equalling them, you may want to think carefully about how the relationship needs to change, or if you want it to continue.

THE BEST WAY TO BREAK UP

If you decide that you want to make a break, these suggestions should help. It's always useful to think through exactly what you want to say beforehand, and be as kind as you can.

1. Tell him face-to-face. An email, a telephone call and most definitely a text are not good ways of ending a relationship. (Forget how you may have been dumped in the past. Have your own standards; don't be influenced by the bad behaviour of others.)

2. Decide precisely what you are going to say – and make sure you say it. If you've really thought it through, you won't be tripped up at the last minute by not being clear.

3. Meet somewhere relatively quiet where you can talk easily. You don't want your ex to think the two of you are off for a weekend in Dover when you are really telling him 'It's over.'

Don't immediately start
looking for another man.
Allow your wounds
to heal and take time
to bathe in the
affection of
your closest friends.

4. If your soon-to-be ex looks blank and uncomprehending, it is OK to call him the next day to make sure he understood what you were saying. Make it clear at the start of the conversation, though, that you are not changing your mind.

5. If you are really concerned about him, ask someone he knows and likes to keep an eye on him. There's no need to get into a long conversation about why you are ending the relationship (unless he or she is a really good friend of yours too, and it would help you to talk). Just make your request and accept that you have acted as well as you could in the circumstances.

♥ *What happens if you get dumped?*

No sane man would want to dump a Sex Kitten, but if your mate doesn't appreciate you and wants to end the relationship, here are the ten Sex Kitten tips for coping with a broken heart.

1. Give yourself a few days (a weekend is ideal) to moan to your girlfriends, play the saddest songs you can find on CD and weep.

2. Then get busy, filling your diary with things you enjoy. Don't immediately start looking for another man. Allow your wounds to heal and take time to bathe in the affection of your closest friends.

3. Take care of yourself by eating well (and that means healthily, by the way – avoid comfort eating and binge-drinking, otherwise you'll end up feeling bad about that too). And get enough sleep. Difficult emotions are easier to handle when you are properly rested and fed. You'll also boost your self-esteem with the knowledge that you are looking after yourself.

4. Accept that it is over. Don't 'accidentally' bump into him in the hope he will see you and change his mind; don't quiz mutual friends about his plans; and NEVER drive past his house and look longingly at the windows. That is borderline stalking. The same applies to ringing his answerphone, just to listen to his voice.

5. Accept that it will hurt. Assuming the relationship has lasted more than six months, you'll have a depth of feeling that can't be erased in a flash (and some people find themselves in the throes of powerful feelings after just six dates).

6. Remember the Sex Kitten's motto – 'I don't need to get my good feelings from someone else. I can find them inside myself.' – and set about clearing your room/flat/loft/house. This means removing all traces of your ex, at least until you are able to look at them and think only of the good times you shared. Anything that produces a twinge of pain is to be put in the back of a cupboard or thrown away, assuming it isn't a pair of diamond earrings you might later regret chucking out with the garbage. (After all, you can always wear his diamonds to the supermarket to cheer yourself up.)

7. Talk to someone who knows you well about what went wrong. Wait until you are feeling better, though. If you start analysing all the reasons for the break-up the minute your partner leaves, your judgement will be clouded by misery and low self-esteem. Leave it until you have accepted he is not coming back. And be prepared to listen to what your friend has to say. He or she may not be offering the entire truth of where you went wrong, but it will be a perspective that isn't yours, and that will be useful in itself.

8. Don't expect to be over it completely in just a couple of weeks. It can sometimes take up to six months to recover from the break-up of

You can
always wear
his diamonds to the
supermarket to
cheer yourself up.

a one-year relationship, and it may be even longer before you are fully ready to put the past entirely behind you.

9. Don't try to stay friends with your ex in the short term. Friendship is about support and the knowledge that someone is there for you. A former partner is not able to offer you that straightaway. Trying to stay friends, especially if one partner is acting out of guilt, will muddy the waters of any friendship that may develop between you at a later stage. Give it at least six months, and ideally a year, before you become friends. Don't be afraid to say 'no' if he asks 'Can we be friends?' straight after the break-up. You'll be doing yourself a favour in the long run.

10. Look for a new relationship only when you are reasonably confident that you understand what went wrong last time. If you dive headlong into something simply because you can't bear to be alone, and before you have worked out why the previous one failed (a mistake made by a lot of men), it may not be long before an unhappy pattern begins to repeat itself.

♥ *A Sex Kitten knows*

♥ how to fall in love without losing herself.

♥ the moment to try harder … and when to walk away.

♥ whom she can trust, whom she can't, and when to give a friend a second chance.

♥ that she can't change the length of her legs, the width of her hips, or the nature of her parents (but she can choose to wear high heels, bias-cut skirts and forgive her family – they were only doing the best they could, after all).

♥ *The single Sex Kitten's must-haves*

♥ a sense of control over her destiny.

♥ a youth she feels fine to leave behind.

♥ a past racy enough to look forward to retelling in old age.

♥ one old love she can imagine going back to … and one who reminds her of how far she has come.

♥ enough money within her control to move out and get a place of her own, even if she never needs to or wants to.

♥ at least one friend who always makes her laugh, and at least one friend who lets her cry.

♥ a set of screwdrivers, a cordless drill and some sizzling black lace underwear (and she knows how to use them all) …

How to talk to your man

Purrs or hisses?

Ever noticed that his eyes glaze over when you tell him 'We need to talk'? Sex Kittens know how to be heard. And that's because they understand one simple fact: communicating with a partner about sex (or anything else for that matter) is so much easier once you decide to ask for what it is you want. Understand also that men are programmed to respond to some of our standard approaches in negative ways and soon you'll be connecting better than ever before ...

Remember a really good conversation that you and your lover enjoyed together. It may have been intensely serious, or you may have laughed a lot. Perhaps he talked first, and then encouraged you to share your thoughts. Perhaps it was the other way around. More than likely there was a balance between you that felt comfortable and easy.

Good sex is essentially a physical extension of that kind of conversation. Sometimes it may feel intense and passionate; other times it may be giggly and fun. But it will always depend on both partners 'saying' what is on their mind and being prepared to give time and attention to each other. When one of you expects always to be entertained by the other, whether it is over the dinner table or in bed together, sooner or later all the love and pleasure drain from the relationship. Yet it takes only a little effort and imagination to light the spark of desire.

♥ *Sharing your needs*

This chapter is about sharing your needs and sexual desires with your partner. That matters for women *and* men because the best sex involves emotional intimacy, which means feeling comfortable being yourself, and sharing more than mundane questions like 'Did you put the rubbish out?' Saying 'Tell me about your day' and *really* listening to the reply is a step towards emotional intimacy, as is talking about your hopes, your feelings and your vision of life together. And you thought good sex meant swinging from a chandelier? Or spending the weekend in bed, staggering only to the fridge or corner shop for sustenance?

Well, of course, it can mean those things too, but don't confuse the lust you usually experience at the beginning of a relationship with the close, intimate sex that comes with an understanding of the way women and men work sexually. It's an easy mistake to make … but Sex Kittens know better.

❤ *Good vibrations*

Sex Kittens have discovered that they must communicate with their partners because their own sexual needs are essentially rather more complex than those of most men.

A man's higher level of testosterone means it is easier for him to be aroused, and a warm, self-lubricating vagina is the ideal place to stimulate a penis. Nature (and we're back to prehistoric times here) designed men to reach orgasm and ejaculate after a few minutes of thrusting, so they could run off and fight predators at the drop of a club, having briefly ensured the survival of their species. It follows that, although most men enjoy variety in lovemaking, few actually require sophisticated techniques in order to reach orgasm. An attractive and willing partner is usually sufficient.

Women are very different. One recent American survey of more than forty thousand married women revealed that almost half of them reported they failed to reach orgasm either frequently or occasionally during intercourse.

Female orgasm is not guaranteed by the act of penetration. Which is why some women can think about shoe-shopping, chocolate or painting their bedroom scarlet while they are having sex. This may make you a great multi-tasker, but it isn't recommended for a fulfilling love life. And don't forget that sex is not just about orgasm, either. Satisfying sex for women is also about intimacy, sharing and warmth. So most women prefer a level of communication in sex beyond a few grunts and groans – even if it is just a chat and a cuddle over a glass of wine afterwards.

Before we blame Mother Nature and chauvinistic men for short-changing women when it comes to sexual pleasure, we need to remember that women were given a part of their anatomy which has no purpose other than to bring them exquisite pleasure – the clitoris. Eve Ensler, author of *The Vagina Monologues*, a theatrical phenomenon that

How are men going to know
what to do unless they get
some guidance? What
worked with a previous
girlfriend may do absolutely
nothing, or even be a
complete turn-off, for
a new partner.

made the word 'vagina' acceptable at dinner parties, quotes from Natalie Angier's *Woman: An Intimate Geography:*

> The clitoris is pure in purpose. It is the only organ in the body designed purely for pleasure. The clitoris is simply a bundle of nerves: 8,000 nerve fibres, to be precise. That's a higher concentration of nerve fibres than is found anywhere else in the body, including the fingertips, lips and tongue, and it is twice … twice … twice the number in the penis. Who needs a handgun when you've got a semiautomatic?

But handguns and semiautomatics come with instructions, and the sexual anatomy of every woman is different (even though some text books still assert that all women are designed the same way). In the late 1950s, a scientist with the glorious name of Kermit Krantz explored the link between women's genitals and their nervous system. He discovered that there was a wide variation in the way nerve endings were distributed throughout the body. And – with due respect to Natalie Angier – although most women had the highest concentration of nerve endings in the clitoris, some had more nerve endings in the labia minora (inner lips of the vulva); equally, while some women had high concentrations of nerve endings in one part of the genitals, others had a more even spread of nerve endings over a wider area.

What this means is that in the same way that no two faces are alike, so each woman has genitals that are unique to her. And, as a result, each woman needs to be stimulated differently to experience sexual pleasure. So how are men going to know what to do unless they get some guidance? What worked with a previous girlfriend may do absolutely nothing, or even be a complete turn-off, for a new partner.

Some clitorises like to be rubbed, sucked and teased; others can hardly stand to be breathed upon. Your partner needs to know what your preferences are. (Some ancient traditions believe there is a link between a woman's upper lip and her clitoris, by the way. The *Kama Sutra* suggests that the man nibbles or sucks her upper lip while she kisses his lower lip. And in Japan shiatsu massage links the upper lip to the digestive and sexual systems and considers that pressure here stimulates sexual desire. Next time you kiss your partner, suck gently on his lower lip, and see for yourself …)

But men are not given this kind of information as a rule. In fact, pornography, which whether we like it or not is the most common starting point for teenage boys learning about sex, offers seriously misleading suggestions about what women want sexually. For a start, women in porn are permanently ready and available for sex; they reach orgasm after being on the receiving end of a few minutes' vigorous thrusting; they are keen to perform oral sex; and they love it when a man ejaculates inside their mouth.

OK, there may be some truth here for some women, but it is not the whole picture for most. No real-life woman is always ready for sex; the majority of women do not climax with vaginal penetration alone; hygiene and cleanliness matter to women who enjoy giving oral sex; and, frankly, for a lot of women the jury is out on the joys of swallowing semen. (About 60 per cent don't swallow, if you were wondering.) When you add the fact that the fast thrusting in pornography is timed to the masturbatory stroke of a man's hand and bears no relation to the variety of movement most women enjoy, it's pretty miraculous so many men manage to be good lovers, considering the minuscule amount of help they get anywhere else.

♥ *Opening dialogue*

Of course, it's all very well having a wonderful pleasure button, but what do you do if it isn't getting pressed? If you've never felt able to communicate well about your sexual needs, how do you begin?

A Sex Kitten knows how to convey her likes and dislikes without making her partner feel he's messing up or missing out. She also knows that communication works better through purrs than hisses. Bearing in mind the Sex Kitten's understanding that sex isn't something outside the rest of your relationship, but an integral part of it, the skills of good communication that apply to the rest of your relationship apply to discussing sexual matters too.

These skills may require a little fine tuning, though, because when it comes to sex even the roughest, toughest guys can be surprisingly vulnerable. Never underestimate your power to wound a man with words. The upside of this is that even a moderate amount of praise from you can make your man feel great. So choose your words carefully when it comes to giving feedback about your sex life together.

You also need to remember that, when it comes to communication, male and female brains are hardwired differently. Women tend to talk to bond with their friends and families, whereas men tend to talk to communicate facts and information. Some researchers believe this also dates back to prehistoric times, when women and children stayed close to the cave and talked in order to build close relationships to survive, while the men went hunting or fishing and no one talked for fear of startling the prey. Even though we now feed ourselves by buying food in supermarkets and there are dads who stay at home to bring up children, we still have some behaviour left over from the times when dinner meant brontosaurus and bush leaves. Men are far happier sitting silently together while fishing, say, whereas women who go shopping together will talk most of the time. And though a female brain can effortlessly process six to eight thousand words a day, a man's capacity for talk can be as little as two to four thousand words.

As women use talk to reward and bond with other people, most women tend to think that doing a lot of talking is the best way to solve difficulties in their relationships. They are right, especially if the problem is with another woman, but this only works up to a point as

Love means something
different to each person;
let your partner establish
what your relationship
means for him,
and don't push for
a commitment to
match your feelings.

far as many men are concerned. Difficulties need to be dealt with, but endless discussion is not the best way forward for most males.

So don't be inclined to begin a discussion about sex with the vague statement 'We need to talk'. This puts the fear of God into most men because they usually perceive it as 'You are doing something wrong, and I am going to tell you all about why you are doing it wrong'. The two other no-nos when it comes to talking to a man about your relationship are 'Do you love me?' and 'What are you thinking?'

No man wants to be pushed into a declaration of love, even if he does love you. And if he doesn't, it is a speedy way to end the relationship. 'I love you' is a powerful statement, and it is weakened if it is dragged out of you before you feel ready to say it, plus it leaves the person forced into saying it feeling cornered and uncomfortable. Also, asking 'Do you love me?' makes the questioner appear needy and insecure. Love means something different to each person; let your partner establish what your relationship means for him, and don't push for a commitment to match your feelings.

To a lesser extent, the question 'What are you thinking?' works the same way for men. They feel trapped because they know that an honest reply probably isn't what you want to hear. Women tend to ask it when they want reassurance that the relationship is OK. And usually they are disappointed with the reply. This is because men mostly aren't thinking about the relationship at all when the question is asked. They might be thinking that their football team needs a new striker or wondering if they should upgrade their computer. Much less of a man's thinking time is devoted to his relationships.

If you want to talk about your relationship (and this applies not just to sex), make that clear and ask your partner if now is a good time. Remember 'Is now a good time to talk?' is infinitely preferable to that hint-of-doom phrase 'We need to talk'. If it isn't a good time for him, don't argue about why you should talk ('But this is important ...'). Simply find another time, preferably in the next twenty-four hours.

If the subject is sex, you will probably find it easier to talk fully clothed and ideally not immediately before you make love. Generally, talking about sexual difficulties when you are undressed is not a good idea because people are more vulnerable when they aren't wearing their clothes. (If you've ever tried to hold a serious conversation with a doctor while you are sliding on your skirt, you'll know what I mean.)

♥ *Suggesting changes*

If you want to suggest changes in your sex life, put in a bit of thinking time on your own first. It might help to focus your thoughts if you make a list of how you would like to be seduced. What you would like your partner to do to get you in the mood for sex; what you can do to get yourself in the mood for sex; how you would like to be aroused to the point of orgasm; what you would like your partner to do when you are on the brink of orgasm and when you actually experience orgasm; and how you would like to be together afterwards.

For example, you might want to hear how much your partner desires you before sex, or you might want to spend time talking together intimately first. To put yourself in the mood, you may want to read an erotic novel, or take a leisurely bubble bath and drink a glass of wine. For arousal to grow, you may want to share a sexual fantasy or be kissed or touched in a certain way. On the brink of orgasm, you may want him to vary the pace and tempo of thrusting, stimulate your clitoris differently, not talk at all; and afterwards you may want to lie in his arms and talk, or open another bottle of champagne … *Don't leave this list lying around and hope he takes the hint!*

One of the main difficulties in communication between men and women is that women tend to make requests by suggesting and hinting, and then become frustrated and angry when their partner does not pick up what they are talking about. And when it comes to sex,

Focus your thoughts
by making a list of how you
would like to be seduced.

women can grow increasingly obscure, sometimes barely mentioning something they would like, or a difficulty they are experiencing, often because they are labouring under the misapprehension that your sexual partner is supposed to know instinctively what to do to turn you on. Or because they fear that somehow they will hurt their partner's feelings. Naturally, it is right to be sensitive to your partner's reactions. But to shut down on your own sexual needs is not the right message to give in your relationship.

Start with something positive Even if you are reaching boiling point – maybe you have been hiding disappointment or anxiety for a while and have finally decided to voice your grievances – don't begin with a negative comment. For example, 'I'm not having orgasms, and sometimes I fake them so you aren't disappointed' would be a shattering blow to your partner. If you can, start by mentioning some part of your sexual relationship that you do like. If you are in despair about your sex life, praise your partner for another aspect of your relationship that works. If none of it works, you need to ask yourself 'Why am I in this relationship at all?'

Avoid criticizing – talk about what you would like instead It can be tempting to begin a discussion about sex with the words 'I don't like …' While this may be perfectly valid, because there are indeed things you don't like, using the phrase will immediately put your partner on the defensive. And someone who is feeling defensive and upset or angry won't be in the most receptive state to listen to your suggestions. The chances are he will simply defend himself, or hit back at you with an 'I don't like' too. So that the opportunity for positive change will be lost. For example, instead of saying 'I don't like the fact that sex is over so fast', you could say 'I really like it when you hold me in your arms afterwards. It makes me feel good as I like feeling close to you. Can we try some other things too?'

Be specific Murmuring about wanting 'more passion' won't get you anywhere. In fact, you may end up worse off, as your partner will probably feel insulted and that he's not measuring up as a lover. In your eyes, that may be the case. But don't just baldly state your problem; imagine the impact on him when he hears the words. The golden rule is probably: 'Don't say anything that would make you feel bad if you heard it yourself.'

But being kind does not mean keeping quiet or wrapping up your message in vague hints. Women tend to say things like 'I want to make love, not just have sex', without explaining what 'making love' means to them. No two people have the same understanding of what it means to make love. A woman who says this probably means she wants more tenderness and consideration from her partner; but that has to be explained, one step at a time. Remember that men begin their exploration of the territory of sex from a different place to women. But give them a map and be prepared to meet them halfway and most will happily join you en route.

What does 'making love' mean to you? Does it mean your partner stroking your hair and looking into your eyes? Is it hearing him say 'I love you' during sex? Is it being kissed all over your body, not just on your mouth? Does it mean your partner running you a bath before sex and tenderly kissing and patting you dry? Work out your definition of making love and then convey it to your partner. And ask for what you *do* want, rather than complaining about what you don't get. So saying 'I'd love it if you kissed my arms and legs' works better than 'Why don't you kiss me anywhere else but on my mouth?'

And if you feel your partner always wants sex more than you, telling him 'Leave me alone. Can't you see I'm not interested?' won't work as well as 'I know sex is important to you, and it is to me too, but the more you talk about it, the less I want it. It would help if you gave me some time to get charged up myself.' When one partner chases after the other for anything, whether it is more intimacy or more sex, the end result is usually that he or she drives that partner further away. Pursuing someone with demands is invariably a strategy that widens the divide between you, rather than narrowing it.

Talk about yourself rather than commenting on your partner It is always tempting to stick labels on other people rather than acknowledge our own responsibility for what is going on in a relationship, whether we are talking about sex or who does the shopping. But saying 'You are lazy – you don't bother to turn me on', not only means you are abdicating responsibility for your pleasure in the relationship, it is also not an effective way to make a man feel he wants to spend hours giving you sexual pleasure. A man on the receiving end of a verbal put-down usually feels humiliated and diminished, and in no state to start investing more time and energy in his relationship. Instead, try saying 'I'd like to spend more time on foreplay so that I can feel really excited. I like the feeling of closeness and the passion it sparks inside me.'

When the temperature starts to rise, cool down Talking about sex makes people feel vulnerable, and when they feel vulnerable, they get defensive. It is only a short step from defensive to angry, and one further small step to aggressive. Take a break if you find yourself caught in a negative spiral of not listening and not understanding as you both keep repeating different versions of the same argument. Agree to stop talking about sex and do something else for a while, either on your own or together. Then agree another time to talk.

Never trade insults. Saying unkind things about people's sexual performance strikes at the heart of who they are. And it's the fastest route to wrecking your sex life for a long time to come. Steer clear of the words 'always' and 'never'. While it may feel as though those words beef up your argument, and on one level they do, just ask yourself what you want the end result of your discussion to be. Do you think you can bludgeon your partner into changing his sexual habits? You can't. Neither can you 'win' a conversation about sex that becomes an argument. The same rules apply to a discussion about sex as to every other kind of interaction. Think 'win–win', and try to find a solution that enables both of you to get something out of it.

Aggression may bring you a short-term gain, but your partner will remain hostile. Conversely, passivity, when you deny your feelings and desires, means you are unlikely to get what you want. Being assertive and communicating clearly, honestly and kindly about your needs is the most effective tactic to build better communication between you.

Allow your partner some space to think and respond Listen to his answer without interrupting. A man who believes his partner genuinely hears his thoughts and respects his views is much more likely to say 'I love you' unprompted. And men, especially, often need time to take on board new ideas about their relationship. Expect them to mull things over for a while before making any changes.

DURING LOVEMAKING

If you aren't sure how to communicate while you are actually making love, bear in mind these three guidelines.

1. Keep it simple.

2. Keep it positive. 'Touch me here' will always be better than 'Don't touch me there'.

3. Non-verbal messages often work best. Noises of encouragement ('mmn' [more please]) and gently placing your partner's hands where you would like them can be more effective than lists of complex instructions that have him struggling to remember what goes where.

♥ *Keeping in touch*

You don't need to talk about your sexual relationship all the time, but it is good to discuss it now and again. This way you can both keep in touch with changes in each other's tastes and desires. After all, once you have found something someone likes, there is a temptation to keep doing it, in the hope you will always be pressing the right buttons. But, in the same way that people can change their opinions, habits and clothes, so they can change their sexual preferences.

If you have never talked about sex, and plenty of couples don't, it may feel awkward or embarrassing when you first bring up the subject. But as long as you make it clear that your desire is to create a better sex life for you both, and to build a stronger relationship between you, the discussions should get easier and be more fun as time goes by.

Sometimes, as the cliché goes, actions speak louder than words, so if you hesitate to talk outright about the best way for your partner to bring you sexual pleasure, suggest giving each other a relaxing hand or foot massage. This is a very unthreatening approach to identifying what brings you pleasure, and you can begin to give gentle feedback on what you like best.

♥ *Playing sexy games*

Games are a great way of building a connection between you and livening up your sexual encounters. Whether it's strip scrabble or a pillow fight, games are about having fun together and revelling in the connection cemented by playful enjoyment of each other's company.

The Please, Please Me Game is usually a winner, and it's a brilliant way of communicating about what you each find pleasurable as well. It's best played when you are warm, comfortable and wearing not much or nothing at all, and it's important to find a relaxed space where you know you won't be interrupted for at least an hour. There are two roles: one person is the receiver; the other is the giver. The giver has to touch, stroke or massage the receiver somewhere on his/her body, and he/she has to give the response 'yes', 'no', 'maybe' or 'please', depending on his/her reaction to the touch. You can split the hour into thirty-minute segments and swap roles halfway through, or opt for a full hour in one role, on the understanding that the next time you will change places.

The joy of this game is that you don't have to use a torrent of words to put across what you like. It also gets couples used to the idea that sex is not just about the genitals, but that the entire body can produce thrilling sexual feelings. Men, in particular, are often surprised at the sensitivity of a woman's skin (which, as I've said before, and will continue to repeat, is around ten times more sensitive than a man's) and it can be a revelation for them to discover that they can bring their partner such pleasure (a) without going anywhere near her vagina, and (b) without using their penis. Fingers, toes and even chest hair stroked across a naked body can create pleasurable sensations.

Some couples extend this game into a massage, and trail silky fabrics or feathers across the skin to heighten sensitivity. Quite apart from the delight this can bring, it helps wake up the senses, and that means that if sex does happen later on, the body is already primed for a heightened experience. Enjoy!

Creating a seductive space

The purrfect place to make love

Never underestimate the link between sensuality and sex. Of course, there's nothing wrong with wild sex under the glare of an overhead bulb, but usually it is much more engaging to opt for a softly lit space which brings pleasure to the eyes and ears, thrills to the skin and delight to the taste buds while smelling divine. Here's how to make your lovemaking truly sensational …

So, how do you create your seductive space? What says 'Sex Kitten'? And what says 'I'm not that fussed about making love with you'? Accepting that all five senses can play a role in a truly satisfying sexual experience, tactile fabrics (touch), soft lighting (sight), champagne and a dish of ripe strawberries (taste and smell) make an inviting playground for a start. Anything that implies you haven't grown up yet – a doll collection or a whole zoo of cuddly toys – is best tidied away.

❤ *Prepare the room*

It need not be a bedroom, especially if yours is stuffed with piles of ironing and mountains of shoes. And if you don't possess any means of playing music there either, you may decide to create your seductive space in your sitting room, say, and enjoy the sound system. But make sure that you will have complete privacy for as long as you need. Flatmates, young children or your teenagers with their gangs of friends need to know when your space is strictly off-limits.

If you can't be certain that the sitting room is a safe haven, do your best to clear away the debris from your bedroom – and fit a lock on the door – so that when you and your partner enter it feels safe, warm and inviting. (If you are a fresh-air enthusiast who keeps bedroom windows open to blast in a chilly breeze, close them now. Bodies tense up if they are cold, and you want to ensure that you feel at your most relaxed.)

You could take a commonsense tip from the *feng shui* experts, who believe unnecessary clutter builds up negative energy and that drags you down mentally and physically. They say the home is overlaid with an energy grid called the *bagua* that reflects all the different aspects of your life and the way you relate to the world around you. The far right-hand corner of each room is said to be the relationship corner, and if all it contains is an old pair of trainers and some frayed knickers, then your relationship may not be in the best possible state …

Whether or not you are a fan of this Chinese philosophy, most of us would agree that our environment affects our awareness. Emotions are stimulated by colours, for example. Research has shown that women are drawn to brighter colours at particular times in their menstrual cycle, and colour therapists believe that certain colours affect our mood and the way we view ourselves and other people.

Certainly, you may recall walking into a room and shivering if the walls were a particularly cold shade of blue or, equally, feeling your spirits rise when you encountered a Mediterranean sunshine yellow. If a quick glance around your home reveals tattered wallpaper, tired curtains and nowhere that looks remotely inviting, you may want to think about decorating your seductive space. Just a string or two of tiny lights round the bedhead and some new linen can perk up a dull room; add a fake-fur throw and some velvet cushions and already it has begun to take on a more inviting feel.

Whether you choose a major or mini makeover, or simply have a quick tidy up, is your decision, of course. The most important thing is that at least occasionally you make a special effort to prepare the place where you and your partner will make love.

❤ *Think about lighting ...*

Whatever the colour of your walls, the way you use lighting in your seductive space is going to be significant. If you are beginning to accept yourself as the gorgeous creature you undoubtedly are, then you are ready for your partner to admire you.

Countless women rush to switch off the light and leap under the bedclothes before their partner sees them naked, but they are depriving themselves and their partner on two counts. Firstly, your partner is missing out on the favourite male pastime of looking at a naked female body (why else do porn magazines sell in their millions?). And

Candlelight
instantly creates
an intimate,
romantic atmosphere,
caressing the skin
with a warm,
gentle glow.

secondly, you are both missing out on the joy of being admired and appreciated ... Remember, men like compliments about their bodies.

Of course, it makes sense to present yourself in the best possible light, which, without a doubt, is candlelight. Apart from the fact that candlelight instantly creates an intimate, romantic atmosphere, it caresses the skin with a warm, gentle glow. The average household electric bulb, by way of contrast, sends out a thin yellow light with a dash of orange in it, and that tints pale naked human skin a distinctly unflattering shade of grey.

Pink and red candles signify passion, but some people prefer the purity of white candles, or the soft flickering of lots of little tea-lights scattered around the room. Scented candles impact on two senses for the price of one, and save you the trouble of burning incense or wafting a room fragrance around beforehand. But always remember to extinguish candles before you fall asleep. You don't want your romantic evening to end with your home going up in smoke.

Research in the United States reported that under blue and green lighting men said that their partner's breasts looked and felt larger, and women said that their partner's penis looked bigger. Tests on college students showed that a red light speeded up erection and green illumination slowed it down. So OK, you could bulk buy coloured bulbs if you are sensitive about physical sizes, but frankly you would probably be wasting your money. One of the biggest (and most persistent) myths around is that a large penis is more sexually satisfying for a woman. It is not.

Generally, women experience most sexual sensation in their clitoris and the first five centimetres of their vagina. If a woman is fully aroused, and her vagina is engorged and therefore at its most responsive, even a man with a very small penis can reach her most sensitive places. The trick is to be fully aroused before a man enters you. For most women this takes a pleasurable twenty to thirty minutes of stimulation by her partner's fingers, lips or tongue. Think of your vagina as being carefully designed to accept penises belonging only to gorgeous men that you find sexy. For a woman who is fully turned on, penis size is irrelevant.

Sadly, very few men understand that penis size is genuinely unimportant and most are caught up in the mistaken belief that bigger is better. Tread carefully when you are explaining that this is not the case, though. Should the question arise, it's probably best to say something tactful and complimentary like 'We are a perfect fit' rather than 'You being small doesn't make any difference.' Some myths are embedded in the male psyche and suggesting a man has a small penis, even with the best of intentions, will deliver a serious blow to his pride. Showing how much you adore his penis will dispel any uncertainties he may have. How you want to demonstrate the way you feel about his pride and joy is up to you, but there probably isn't a man on the planet who does not adore receiving oral sex. (See page 120 for the Sex Kitten's *pièce de résistance*.)

❤ *... and music*

Long before Shakespeare wrote 'If music be the food of love, play on', couples fell in love to music, treasured their own special songs, and even parted to a backdrop of music that probably had the power to make them cry, sometimes years afterwards. Music can bypass the rational side of the brain and speak directly to the heart, which is why choosing to make love with music playing in the background can greatly enhance sexual experience.

Twenty years ago, the scene in the movie *'10'* in which Dudley Moore famously seduced Bo Derek to the accompaniment of Ravel's *Boléro* struck a chord with cinema audiences as they witnessed the rise of physical passion between the lovers match that long, long musical crescendo. People who had never before associated classical music with sex flocked to record stores and for a while that piece became the musical score for lovemaking all over the world.

The act of listening to music also has a physiological effect. Certain types of music slow your brain waves and as a result you feel calmer and more relaxed; and your skin becomes more sensitive to touch and temperature. Music played at around sixty beats a minute even has the ability to lower heart rate, breathing and brain waves to the same levels as those experienced in meditation. (Popular classical music, including pieces by Mozart, Tchaikovsky and Chopin, light jazz and most New Age music generally play at this tempo.) Rock music, on the other hand, tends to be much faster and causes your brain waves to cycle faster too, making you want to speed up whatever you are doing. So play rock if you fancy some fast, flamboyant sex …

❤ *What will you eat?*

Food and sex are two of life's greatest pleasures and go well together, as long as you avoid the pitfall of eating a heavy meal before you make love. If you do succumb to that temptation, your body will need to focus on digesting, and you'll probably feel bloated and unsexy as a result. But don't let this put you off eating with your partner before sex. As the editors of all those glossy cookery books know, the enjoyment of food can be an incredibly sensual experience.

Try taking a picnic to bed or wherever you choose to make love. Bite-sized pieces of fruit are best; strawberries, grapes, raspberries and bananas all work well, dipped in champagne or wine. Take turns in feeding each other, gently brushing your partner's lips with the fruit before you slide it into his mouth. American scientists have discovered that women are turned on by the aroma of cucumber (one study revealed it boosted their production of testosterone) and liquorice, and men go wild for the smell of pumpkin pie. See for yourself.

A partly clothed body is
much more alluring
than a completely naked one –
even if the only items
you are wearing are a
necklace and earrings.

❤ *What will you wear?*

Most people think that the whole point of sex is to get your clothes off, and to some extent they are right. But a partly clothed body is much more alluring than a completely naked one – even if the only items you are wearing are a necklace and earrings.

The secret of what to wear for sex is to wear what makes *you* feel sexy. Even if it isn't your partner's first choice of clothing for you, it won't matter because what men want is a woman who is turned on – not a woman who is wearing something to please them that she actually finds deeply uncomfortable. If you are not sure what makes you feel sexy, have fun and experiment.

Go shopping with a girlfriend – or with your partner – and try on different styles of underwear. Of course, buy something you feel comfortable in, but keep an adventurous spirit. More and more female-friendly stores in town centres are specializing in sex toys and sexy clothes for women. The sales assistants are generally polite, matter of fact and friendly. Pop in to see if you can find something that you like. They are great places for a giggle too. Sex shouldn't be an obligation or a burden, and focusing on your sense of playfulness can banish unhelpful worries.

Regard dressing up for sex as one way of bringing the fun back into your sexual relationship. If you and your partner enjoy playing out sexual fantasies, you probably have a wardrobe full of appropriate playwear already. If you've just wondered what it might be like, talk to your partner and see if it appeals to him *before* you invest in your nurse's uniform or the leather dominatrix outfit. One word of warning, though: some people find that certain fantasies are best kept inside their head. Acting them out leaves them feeling embarrassed and vaguely let down. But give it a go – if you've a robust sexual relationship, you'll find you can cope with the occasional disappointment. And it might get the sparks flying.

♥ *The power of perfume*

Our sense of smell has a direct effect on our emotional reactions. This is because any scent picked up by the olfactory nerve makes an impact on the brain immediately, while food and drink have to enter the bloodstream before the body can react to them fully. An unpleasant smell can turn you off quicker than you can wrinkle your nose in disgust. An appealing smell, however, can play a powerful role in making you feel aroused. Which is why the million-dollar fragrance industry will never go out of business.

Sure, your skin produces its own unique scent. Remember the pheromones that attract people to you (see page 48)? But you can top it up with an array of other scents to enhance your own sexual experience. Be aware, though, that every skin has its own pH balance – or acid/alkali ratio – and that it varies according to mood and temperature. Which is why the same perfume smells differently on different people at different times. So don't invest a fortune in the scent that makes your best friend smell gorgeous without trying it on your own skin. (There's at least one fragrance that smells heavenly on a friend of mine but has the distinct aroma of lavatory cleaner on me.) It takes at least ten minutes for your skin chemicals to react with a scent so, when you are choosing a new perfume, don't be seduced by the smell in the tester bottle. Try it and wander around the store for a while before making a final decision.

A smoker's skin doesn't hold perfume for as long as that of a non-smoker. Dry skin allows perfume to evaporate faster than oily skin. Sweat washes away perfume, but hot, muggy weather increases the impact of your fragrance much more than cool, dry weather, so go easy in the summer. Dousing yourself in perfume can be overpowering and have the opposite effect to the one you intended.

Finally, if you adore a particular perfume, don't keep it in your cupboard for ages and eke it out a drop at a time. Time, as well as extreme heat or cold, can destroy the delicate balance of oils, fixative and alcohol that makes up its unique fragrance, and you may find yourself with three-quarters of a bottle of something that smells vile after a couple of years.

❤ *Prepare your mind too*

As you create your perfect sexy space – warm, inviting, fun and smelling as gorgeous as you do – think about the erotic encounter to come. Allocating mental space as you physically prepare for sex is a way of charging up your brain with sexual thoughts. Because most of us lead such busy lives, we spend a lot of time unconsciously blocking these thoughts in favour of work or family-related tasks (or both). This means that when we want to be sexual we have to dig deep beneath an avalanche of day-to-day preoccupations and stresses to arouse an erotic response.

In another age, the Indian upper classes for whom the *Kama Sutra* was written enjoyed sex because they took time to focus on it as a relaxing way to spend their leisure (just as people regard TV today). The difference is that by turning sex into a hobby they enriched their relationships in ways that watching the soaps with a partner never will.

Sexy frolics or spiritual intensity?

You choose

Real Sex Kittens know the secret of how to build increasing levels of passion as time goes by. Their bedroom games are not just about fun but also about sexual and emotional fulfilment. Creating a sexual relationship that will last a lifetime owes nothing at all to chance or fate. It is about understanding the role that intimacy plays between you and your partner ...

Let's be honest: for women, the experience of sex can range from the mind-blowing to the barely noticeable. We know that it is perfectly possible for a woman to make love while she thinks about a thousand other things that have absolutely nothing to do with her partner and the sexual situation she is in.

Some women become so cut off from their own sexuality that sex is something in which they rarely feel truly involved. They may do it to please their partner, or to convince themselves that their relationship is OK. But ask them if they really enjoy sex and their honest reply is likely to be 'not much'. The problem with this approach is that in time it prompts a downward spiral, with sex becoming something they find less and less enjoyable.

It's an easy trap to fall into. If you are a woman who restricts herself to trying to keep up with the male sprint towards orgasm, sooner or later you are bound to lose interest in having sex. That, of course, is because the female's instinctive experience of sex is best encapsulated by words like intimacy, variety, sharing, changes in pace, and even humour. Men, by contrast, can get very single-minded and serious about the subject. Often this is because they feel they are solely responsible for the couple's experience. And if performance anxiety sets in as well it can rapidly diminish their pleasure, and usually that of their partner too.

But if together you've sometimes enjoyed the kind of astonishing, wildly exciting and passionate sex that leaves both of you fizzing with delight for days, you'll want to recapture that magic. So what are the essential ingredients that can turn a frankly dull and routine encounter into a memorable one?

Let's look at this in two stages. The first part of the chapter deals with how to have more fun using your current sexual practices, or how to add sparkle to what you are doing already. The second shows you how to change things if you would like to build a deeper and more spiritual approach to your lovemaking.

♥ *The art of kissing*

Very few sex guides mention kissing – most concentrate on sexual positions – but for the majority of women a passionate kiss, delivered really well, turns them on far more than the prospect of having sex upside down. If your partner is a disappointment when it comes to kissing, don't sidestep the issue and give up. People can learn to do things differently. Usually they just require some gentle guidance.

Rather than being tempted to announce one day 'You're not a very good kisser' (which will get you nowhere), think about ways you can develop your own kissing technique. There's a whole lot more to erotic kissing than sticking your tongue down your partner's throat. It's a skill most of us need to learn. It takes time and, ideally, lots of practice. (In China, couples never kiss in public: they regard kissing as something so intimate it would be the equivalent of making love in public.)

If you are planning a real kissathon, clean teeth (remember to floss regularly), no strong smelling food (unless you both adore garlic, say) and clean hands (see below!) will probably be appreciated.

Use your lips and tongue to explore your partner's mouth gently. Run your tongue softly around the inside of his lips, and build slowly towards taking it in turns to suck each other's tongue (some people find this incredibly arousing). And here's where the clean hands come in. Try sliding a finger slowly inside his mouth so that he can suck gently on it. Sucking a thumb or forefinger can feel very erotic, not just because of its resemblance to oral sex, but also because the fingers are blessed with thousands of sensitive nerve endings.

Limiting yourself to kissing your partner's mouth can become routine so use your tongue to explore your lover's face too. You can lick his eyelids, his ears and the underside of his chin, which remains an unexplored erogenous zone for many people.

Sometimes couples, especially those in long-term relationships, practically give up kissing, unless it is going to lead to full-blown sex.

Touch

takes you

instantly back to

the world of

physical response.

They are missing out on so much fun! Kissing isn't just for teenagers; it's a great way to bond with your partner and bring each other mutual pleasure. Sex Kittens know that a kiss can convey all kinds of different messages – from 'You turn me on' to 'I've missed you'. But the most important one is 'You matter to me and I want to be physically intimate with you'. And that is a message no man can ignore.

♥ *The importance of touch*

It might seem like stating the obvious, but massage is a wonderful way to begin a sexual encounter because it connects you with your body. So many women live almost entirely in their heads – analysing problems, planning for work and children, and worrying about picking up the shopping. Touch takes you instantly back to the world of physical response and, if it is done with loving attention, massage is a great way of reconnecting with your partner too.

Always use a massage oil of some sort. Dry hands don't glide across the skin, and if you have slightly rough hands *and* don't use oil, the sensation won't be at all pleasant. Massage with scented oil is even better because it combines the senses of touch and smell.

Use a few drops of good-quality essential oil (rather than the cheaper, chemical counterparts), diluted in some kind of vegetable carrier oil, such as grapeseed or almond. Essential oils are distilled from a wide range of natural sources, including flowers, herbs, fruits and the bark of trees. They can be surprisingly potent; always follow instructions on the labels and don't use more than three at a time or the effect will be overpowering. (Avoid them altogether if you are, or think you might be, pregnant.)

If you are looking for essential oils to bring a certain something to lovemaking, bear in mind that sandalwood is believed to stir sensual feelings, as well as calming the mind. Jasmine is linked to male sexuality, and the scent of rose is associated with femininity. Ylang-ylang is the aroma most widely promoted for its power to stir erotic feelings, but its appeal is not universal. And there's no point persevering with massage oil – or scented candles – in the mistaken belief they will work some magic if your instant reaction when you smell them is 'yuck'. Choose aromas that make your toes curl with delight and, when you have settled on a few favourites, store them in a cool, dark place.

While we are lingering over the prospect of divine smells, never forget that for most people clean bodies are sexier than grubby ones. It's fine to build up a sweat through making love (remember the phrase 'steamy sex'?), but for most of us living in the West in the 21st century and accustomed to daily showers or baths the prospect of kissing clean skin is more appealing than being confronted by stale smells. And it is much more flattering to your partner to shower or bath before making love than not to bother. Rushing to get clean afterwards sends a very different message, though. Saying 'I want to be clean for you' is much more positive than 'I want to wash you off my body as soon as I can'.

Of course, there are fashions in cleanliness, like everything else. In the early 19th century, for example, the Emperor Napoleon sent a letter instructing his beloved Josephine: 'Home in five days – don't wash.' So if cleanliness is not your thing, check your partner feels the same way.

How to give a great massage

It's important to warm your hands and the massage oil before you begin, so stand the bottle of oil in a bowl of warm water, and wash your hands in warm water too. The best place for a massage, assuming you don't have a proper couch, is on the floor so that you can move around freely. (You can't give a good massage if you are feeling twisted and awkward.) Make a welcoming space for your lover – on a rug or blanket covered with a sheet – and use another sheet or towel to cover up parts of the body that aren't being massaged so that he doesn't get cold. If you are in bed together, just modify the moves so you stay comfortable.

1. Begin by massaging his back, focusing in turn on small areas, such as his shoulder blades, upper back, lower back and buttocks, and then slide your fingers down both sides of his spine (being careful not to apply pressure to the spine itself). Vary the strokes you use and, as a general rule, repeat each type three times before gliding into another.

2. When he is melting into the floor, turn your attention to his legs. Massage each leg, first upwards and then very gently downwards. His inner thighs are one of his most erogenous zones so linger longer here. To release tension, and caress the most sensitive part of his legs, use your thumbs to push gently along the backs of his legs (where the seam would be if he were wearing seamed stockings). Then massage his feet, including his toes.

3. Ask him to turn onto his back in his own time, and begin massaging his shoulders, neck and arms, not forgetting his wrists, hands and fingers. Feel free to add gentle kisses all over his body. Some people adore silky fabrics or feathers stroked slowly across their skin too. Tease him with your hair, if it's long, trailing it across his body, use your nipples to swirl patterns on his skin, and never underestimate the impact of soft eyelashes fluttered around his neck and ears.

4. Focus on his abdomen – though not everyone likes being touched here so be sensitive to his reactions – and then the fronts of his legs, again massaging upwards and lastly very gently downwards. Impress him with your knowledge of the 'Rushing Door' Chinese acupuncture pressure point. It lies halfway along the crease at the top of the thigh – where it meets his torso. Hold your first two fingers there for at least sixty seconds. It boosts sexual energy and makes for longer, lustier sex.

117

What men truly adore
is watching a woman who
is bold and enthusiastic
about their penis.

Some people love having their scalp massaged, especially if they are not fussed about their hair getting messy. And the ears are often neglected. According to Chinese traditional medicine, they are filled with acupuncture points, and most ears adore a little loving attention, whether being caressed with fingers and thumb, teeth, lips, a tongue, or just warm breath.

Whisper approvingly as you touch the parts of your partner's body that you particularly like. But be sensitive to his needs. If he says that he wants to relax in total silence, respect his wishes. Hold on to the thought that you want to give him love and pleasure, and that's just what he'll receive.

❤ *All you need to know about oral sex*

If you're not sure how to drive him wild with your lips and tongue, don't be nervous. You are in charge. Most men are more than delighted by the prospect of oral sex and it would take a real killjoy to moan about your technique. On the other hand, being reasonably confident of your skills will make giving your partner pleasure a more enjoyable experience for you, so here are some useful tips.

SEVEN WAYS TO IMPROVE YOUR TECHNIQUE

1. Are you both comfortable? If he is on the bed, ask him to lie on the edge nearest you, so that you can kneel on a cushion or pillow on the floor and reach his penis with ease.

2. Maintain eye contact throughout. For some men this is the sexiest part of oral sex. Although they relish the delicious physical sensations, what they truly adore is watching a woman who is bold and enthusiastic about their penis.

3. Run your fingers through his pubic hair before you begin – you don't want any stray hairs to get stuck in your teeth. Cover your teeth with your lips – some men enjoy the sensation of teeth gliding *very* lightly up and down their penis, but the majority will panic if you bare your teeth at the start!

4. Hold the base of his penis securely by creating a ring with the fingers of one hand as you begin to wrap your lips around the top. Some women are fearful of gagging – by holding the penis as you take it into your mouth, you give your man the impression that you are going down on him more deeply, thus intensifying his pleasure. Holding the base also means you stay in control of how deep you go. Some men enjoy a long string of pearls (already warmed by being worn around your neck) wrapped around their penis and rolled slowly up and down between your cupped hands.

5. Don't just use the tip of a pointed tongue; allow it to flatten and use the underside as well. Pay special attention to the frenulum – a particularly sensitive spot that lies just below the ring of tissue that delineates the tip of his penis. In some men, it can be felt as a small bump; in others there is no physical evidence of it, so be prepared to ask where the best place is to stimulate. If you are too shy to ask outright, put your forefinger in his mouth and ask him to mimic what he'd like you to do with his penis. Don't ignore his testicles – but check with your man that he likes to be touched here first.

6. If inspiration deserts you, imagine you are eating an ice-cream. Begin by licking the shaft of his penis before you take it into your mouth. Go slowly and take your time. You are in charge.

7. Remember your *pièce de résistance.* Your partner's prostate gland plays an important role in male sexuality, and some men adore

By holding the penis as you take it into your mouth, you give your man the impression that you are going down on him more deeply … Holding the base also means you stay in control of how deep you go.

receiving stimulation here, either from the outside or internally. You can massage the prostate via the anus (cleanliness and clipped fingernails are essential, of course) or from the outside, through the perineum, which is the stretch of skin between the testicles and anus. Gently rub his perineum, just in front of his anus, and your man may melt with pleasure. (Pressure here can also stop a man's ejaculation without affecting his ability to experience an orgasm.) This is a centuries-old sex secret that every Sex Kitten should know …

And as for the question 'To swallow or not to swallow?' The main ingredient in semen is naturally occurring sugar fructose and there are around six calories in the average ejaculation, so it's not bad for you and you won't put on weight. As a rule, men love it when you swallow their semen as it makes them feel accepted and appreciated. But it remains, quite literally, a matter of personal taste, and if you decide that swallowing is not for you, there are plenty of other ways of demonstrating that you feel good about him. Only the most insecure man will make a big deal about it.

♥ *Exercising your love muscle*

Your physical sexual equipment is much like any other equipment you use regularly. Take care of it, have some understanding of how it works, and usually you will be rewarded with good service. But while some women spend hours in the gym toning their arms, legs and stomachs, they neglect to exercise the most sexually important muscle in their body, one that can bring them hours of pleasure – the pubococcygeus (PC) muscle. This is also known as the 'love muscle' because tensing it during lovemaking tightens the grip of the vagina on the penis. And it is one of the main movers and shakers during the pulsations of an orgasm. Ignore it at your peril.

The vagina is supported by a group of muscles called the pelvic-floor muscles. These are arranged like a figure-of-eight (or, more poetically speaking, butterfly wings) around the vagina, urethra and anus. The largest of these muscles is the PC muscle, and it connects the front of the pelvis to the lower spine. If you are not sure where to locate yours, it is the muscle you rely on when you are desperate to go to the loo, but need to hold on. It is also the muscle you use to stop the flow of urine. Try it out and see.

If you've had a baby, the PC was the muscle you were most aware of as you pushed, and you were probably told to exercise it after the birth to prevent incontinence. It's unlikely your midwife also pointed out its importance in your sex life, but exercising your PC muscle can be one of the simplest and most effective ways of physically improving your sexual response. And you don't have to go to a gym to do it.

Stage 1 Try tightening and relaxing your PC muscle in short bursts. Tighten as you inhale, and relax as you breathe out. If this earns you odd looks at the bus stop, just tighten and relax the muscle while breathing naturally. Do it twenty times a day. Some women find deciding to do it every time they wash their hands a useful reminder.

Stage 2 Don't try this until you think you've got the hang of Stage 1. When you have, progress to tightening with the in-breath, then retaining the breath for six seconds and bearing down as you exhale. (Your bedroom is probably a better location for this than the bus stop.) To feel a noticeable benefit when you make love, you'll need to practise for several minutes a day. It takes a couple of weeks to begin to tone the PC muscle, and then you are likely to notice a significant difference in your sex life (and you'll have better bladder control).

If you are extra keen to obtain the benefits of exercising the PC muscle, try at least thirty repetitions a day and you'll notice the difference within a week. Do be careful though. Like all muscles, if you overuse it, the PC muscle will become sore and uncomfortable, and you'll defeat the object of the exercise.

It can also help if you imagine you are receiving your partner's penis when you are making love rather than being entered by it. This may sound like meaningless wordplay, but there is a principle at work here. It is about reducing a woman's tendency towards passivity during sex, something that benefits men and women alike, and changing your attitude to penetration plays its part. You'll feel more engaged in the sexual act and, as a result, much sexier.

♥ *Massaging your breasts*

Why should you massage your own breasts, you may be thinking, when it is much more pleasurable to have your partner do it for you? The simple answer is that either works well. Women who experience this type of massage every day claim many benefits – in particular, increased sexual sensitivity in their breasts. This does make sense because you are stimulating nerve endings in the nipple and the rest of the breast, and, if you massage using a deliciously scented body lotion, you are stirring two of your senses at the same time. Some women have extremely sensitive breasts and can reach orgasm through stimulation of their nipples alone.

Begin by rubbing the palms of your hands together to warm them and get the energy flowing. Using the tips of the index, second and third fingers of both hands, move your right hand clockwise and your left hand counter-clockwise around your breasts, slowly and gently pressing against your ribcage. Do this for a couple of minutes, noticing – and enjoying – the pleasurable sensations it will bring. (If you find a lump or anything unusual in your breast, consult your doctor straightaway, of course.)

Even if your breasts are often tender, it may still make sense to give very gentle daily breast massage a try. Begin after your period, when your breasts are at their most comfortable, and continue for the rest of your cycle. (Incidentally, one of the side benefits is lighter periods.)

❤ *How to have an orgasm*

You don't have to experience an orgasm every time you make love. But if you've never had one, it is certainly worth investing a little time to find out what all the fuss is about.

If masturbating by hand (see page 25) or oral sex with your partner has never delivered an orgasm for you, try using a vibrator. The best buy for a novice is one that allows specific clitoral stimulation. The Rabbit, with its small, clitoris-stimulating attachment, was made famous by the girls on TV's *Sex and the City*, and is a bestseller for a very good reason. It works for nearly everyone. But do make sure you use a good-quality lubricant at the same time (see page 126). You can also use a vibrator set to 'low' on other areas of your body, say your breasts, neck or inner thighs, to discover new erogenous zones.

(Some men have incredibly sensitive nipples, by the way, and a vibrator used here or against their testicles sends them skywards into ecstasy. If he is put off the penis-shape of the Rabbit, investigate other options as vibrators come in all sorts of shapes and sizes. The website www.emotionalbliss.com is an excellent source of vibrators that look so innocent you could leave them out on a coffee table.)

Not only do women experience orgasms differently from men, but each woman experiences them differently from every other woman. And each orgasm will be different, depending on a woman's physical, mental and emotional state.

Let's begin by confronting a few myths. All women have a virtually limitless capacity for orgasm, but not all women are multi-orgasmic or even singly orgasmic at the drop of a hat. Most women can reach orgasm by stimulating their clitoris – either with their hand or with a vibrator – but some women require no genital stimulation at all. They can build up to an orgasm through sexually pleasurable feelings elsewhere in the body and occasionally just by the power of the mind. Women can come while riding a horse, in a yoga class or even travelling on the tube (though admittedly this is a rare skill).

The best position in which to achieve an orgasm when you are making love is for the woman to go on top, and the addition of a little manual stimulation of the clitoris at the same time usually pays dividends. Alternatively, suggest to your partner that he changes his pattern of thrusting. If he has a tendency just to plunge in and out, you may not be receiving optimum stimulation in your vagina. The term 'screwing' gives a clue here because the action of slowly grinding in small circles tends to be the one that brings most pleasure to women. Suggest you experiment and see what works for you.

And don't forget the lubricant. One of the Sex Kitten's best friends, it should always be within arm's reach when you make love with your partner. Even though you manufacture your own lubrication inside the vagina, masturbation and penetration are usually much more enjoyable with the help of a little extra lube. Equally, most men are pleasantly surprised at the physical difference that using lubricant can make for them. Use a water-based product (such as KY lubricant, available in most supermarkets) rather than a refined or natural oil-based one (such as Vaseline or massage oil). Oil-based products will damage a latex condom in less than sixty seconds and used in or near the vagina they will block its natural ability to clean itself, which in turn can be the cause of irritating infections.

Incidentally, some women find that making love during their period is more pleasurable because the vagina is especially lubricated and natural swelling helps create a more intense orgasm. If you do want to make love, then it is usually better to go on top of your partner, as it allows a downward flow. While not strictly speaking in the category of improving your sex life, this is one way of improving your general health directly through sex, though probably something your mother didn't mention. Orgasm can reduce, or even eradicate, period pains because it reduces cramps.

So, instead of moaning about your period, try regarding it as a sign of your womanliness and fertility. And don't assume that your partner won't want to make love with you. Fewer men than you might think are bothered by a little blood, and if you are especially worried about staining your Egyptian cotton sheets, just put a towel underneath you and throw it in the washing machine afterwards.

Practise 'letting go' in other areas of your life too. Take your partner or a friend on a roller-coaster ride that has you screaming with fright, dance wildly round the living room, or allow yourself to cry with laughter. All these positive responses will help to hardwire your brain for the letting-go experience of orgasm.

It is also worth asking your doctor if any medication you are taking could be affecting your sexual response. Many antidepressants restrict your ability to experience orgasm, and even some over-the-counter flu remedies can zap your libido.

One final word about orgasm – RELAX. Most women tense up as they feel orgasm approach and 'will' it to happen. In fact, the sensations will be far more intense (yes, that's possible!) *and* last longer if you relax and breathe deeply. As you feel your body start to pulse, breathe slowly, relaxing your tummy muscles, and allow yourself to slide more deeply into the sensation. This is probably the opposite of what you are accustomed to doing, but it should make a remarkable difference.

You may find it hard to relax your stomach muscles fully at first. Many women are so fixated on the idea that they should have a flat stomach that they feel compelled to hold their stomach muscles in whenever they are naked or partially clothed. There are two points to remember here. The first is that women, unlike men, are not designed to have flat stomachs. A woman's belly should be gently rounded. And the second? Many men report that a softly rounded female stomach is far more sexually appealing than a woman with a six-pack.

If you are not convinced, and you still can't manage to relax your tummy muscles when you are walking about, do at least try when you are lying down. Gravity will be in your favour anyway, and breathing deeply into your belly will make a really positive difference to your enjoyment of sex.

♥ *You want more?*

Now let's think about new ways of approaching sex with your partner if you want to build more sexual intimacy between you. The word 'intimacy' has its roots in the Latin word for 'innermost' and many women yearn for a different, more intimate kind of sex beyond the routine of Friday-night shags when you are both worn out. Simply wishing, however, won't make it happen.

Intimate sex is not just something that happens between two sets of genitals. It is about sharing yourself on a different level. If you want to experience sex differently, you can't expect to carry on doing what you are doing. Making changes is vital, yet lots of women don't appreciate this simple fact. They expect to carry on with the same routines, and then are disappointed when their negative feelings and experiences never change. So what are the first steps you can take if you want more meaningful sex?

1. Most importantly, don't try to change everything at once.

2. Begin by concentrating on connecting with your partner in ways that aren't to do with your genitals. Have fun with him outside the bedroom and it's much more likely things will hot up inside it too.

Intimate sex is not just something that happens between two sets of genitals. It is about sharing yourself on a different level.

3. When you *are* naked, remember that many women need up to half an hour of foreplay before they are fully aroused and ready to experience intercourse.

 4. If you want your body to work in your favour, make love in the afternoon, when sex hormones are usually at their peak.

Making love without being naked

This technique sounds rather unlikely, but try it and you may be very pleasantly surprised by its impact. It gives you a real connection, helping to build intimacy and closeness. Incidentally, it's fine to giggle the first time you try it. Some people find making this sort of connection embarrassing simply because they are moving beyond a purely physical process to one that engages their heads and hearts.

1. Sit facing your partner, ideally cross-legged on the floor, so you are physically close.

2. Reach out and place your left hand on the centre of his chest, and allow him to place his left hand on the centre of your chest. Both of you cover your partner's left hand with your right hand.

3. Look into each other's left eye and synchronize your breathing.

Or cuddle up in the 'spoons' position Both lie on your side, with one of you tucked into the back of the other. The person on the 'outside' can wrap an arm around the other. Then synchronize your breathing. You can use either of these positions before or after making love too.

I'm emphasizing the importance of breathing together if you want to intensify your sexual encounter because breathing techniques are hugely underestimated when it comes to sex. If you alter your breathing pattern, you can alter your state of mind. Most of us breathe shallowly and irregularly throughout our lives, using less than a third of our lung capacity. This means we take in only a relatively small amount of oxygen. As a result, our bodies don't function at their optimum level – it is as though we don't have enough octane in our fuel mix. This leads to a build-up of toxins in the body and low energy levels.

For your partner, there is an added advantage in using deep breathing during sex. It will help him be more in control of his arousal rate and give him more choice over when he ejaculates. This is because breathing is connected to heart rate. If you breathe quickly and shallowly, your heart rate increases. If you breathe deeply and slowly, it decreases. Usually, a man breathes twice as fast during sex. This speeds up his heart rate and boosts his need to ejaculate. Deliberate, deep breathing slows the process.

If you aren't sure what deep breathing feels like, watch a film or read a book that makes you laugh out loud. Laughing allows your abdomen to relax and play its proper role in breathing naturally.

LOOK INTO HIS EYES AS YOU REACH ORGASM

Once you have mastered deep breathing during sex, you may want to think about the way you make eye contact. Most people tend to close their eyes in order to concentrate on their physical sensations, which is fair enough. But if you want to develop a deeper connection with your partner, eye contact is crucial.

Looking directly into your partner's eyes as he makes love with you usually evokes a powerful response. And it's even more intimate to look into his eyes as you experience orgasm. Generally, people shut their eyes tight and disappear into a world of their own when they are on the brink of orgasm. Deliberately keeping your eyes open and looking directly at your partner is an incredibly intimate act. Try it and see.

The *Kama Sutra* outlines a practice that has been delighting women for centuries. Known as the Thrusts of the Phoenix, it requires the man to thrust shallowly for nine strokes and then once very deeply.

♥ *Which position?*

Although Sex Kittens know there is far more to sex than changing positions, it is worth spending a few moments considering the most popular sexual positions and the benefits they can bring you as a woman, as well as the ways you can use them to build sexual intimacy.

Woman on top This allows you to look into each other's eyes and kiss while you make love. And, as mentioned earlier, on top is the best position for a woman to experience an orgasm while making love because orgasm for the majority of women is more readily achievable via clitoral stimulation than penetration. Here, with the tip of the penis kept in the most sensitive outer five centimetres of the vagina, male or female fingers can stimulate the clitoris.

Man on top If your partner rests on his hands or elbows, he is more able to control his thrusting technique. The *Kama Sutra* outlines a practice that has been delighting women for centuries. Known as the Thrusts of the Phoenix, it requires the man to thrust shallowly for nine strokes and then once very deeply. Assuming your man can count (and if he can remember a football score he can manage this), you may find this one is a winning combination for you both. And, of course, it also allows you to make eye contact and kiss as you make love. Put a pillow under your hips and it will alter the tilt of your pelvis and expose the clitoris to more friction, boosting the chance of achieving an orgasm.

Man from behind Although you are denied eye contact, this position can be very arousing for both sexes because your vagina will be especially tight. If you want to make it tighter still, press your thighs together and tense your PC muscle (see page 122). If you believe you have a G-spot (and not all women are convinced they do), this is the best position for the penis to reach it.

Never heard of the G-spot? It is named after Ernest Grafenberg, the German gynaecologist who discovered it. Situated a few centimetres inside the vagina, it feels slightly spongy and swells during sexual arousal. The jury is still out on how much of a part it plays in the female orgasm. Some women claim it is the source of fantastic orgasms; others say they barely notice it is there. To find it, insert a finger and make a beckoning or 'come here' motion. During orgasm some women expel a clear fluid from the G-spot through the urethra. This is not the same as urinating, although sometimes women panic and confuse the two. It's what is known as 'female ejaculation'.

Side by side If you want to feel closer emotionally, this is an excellent position, although it can be difficult for your partner to maintain an erection as penetration tends to be rather shallow. Nevertheless, it is a very good way of connecting, whether you lie face to face or in the 'spoons' position.

Scissors This is another position in which you can look into each other's eyes. To replicate the shape of an open pair of scissors with your bodies, lie on your back to the left of your partner while he places his right leg between yours and his left leg underneath you. It's more complicated to describe than it is to do …

Sitting opposite You both need to be reasonably flexible to maintain this position for any length of time, but couples that are fit enough swear that it is one of the best ways of building sexual intimacy. Your partner sits cross-legged and you sit astride him with legs partially around his back. You look into his eyes and both of you rock your pelvises so there is some movement of the penis inside the vagina. Hold each other close and synchronize your breathing. To gain maximum benefit, spend an hour or so on foreplay and penetration before you switch to this position.

But, more important than any position, if you want to make a deep and lasting connection with your lover, you need to shift focus from 'me' to 'us'. This can best be summed up by the thought 'What can I do to show this person how deeply I care for him? How much love and pleasure can I give?' If you *both* approach sex with this in mind, you are almost certainly building a more intimate bond between you.

Tailpiece

Being a Sex Kitten is
not just about dressing in clothes that make you
feel good, getting a wiggle in your walk
and becoming more sensual and
sexy on the outside.
It is about finding
fun and energy
inside *to fuel*
fulfilling relationships
with men and
women. It is
about having
the confidence
to share your
sexiness with
another person
on a deep and
intimate level.
And it is
about taking
delight
in who
you
really
are.

Further reading

Cox, Tracey. *Hot Sex*: *How to Do It*. LONDON: CORGI BOOKS, 1999.

    Supersex. LONDON: DORLING KINDERSLEY, 2002.

    Superflirt. LONDON: DORLING KINDERSLEY, 2003.

Ensler, Eve. *The Vagina Monologues*. LONDON: VIRAGO PRESS, 2001.

Everett, Flic. *Sex Tips for Girls*. LONDON: CHANNEL 4 BOOKS, 2002.

Friday, Nancy. *My Secret Garden: Women's Sexual Fantasies*. LONDON: QUARTET BOOKS, 2002.

Hanauer, Cathi (ed.). *The Bitch in the House*. LONDON: VIKING (PENGUIN GROUP), 2001.

James, Judi. *Sex Signals*. LONDON: PIATKUS, 2003.

Lowndes, Leil. *How to Make Anyone Fall in Love With You*. LONDON: HARPERCOLLINS, 1997.

Sampson, Val. *Tantra: The Art of Mind-Blowing Sex*. LONDON: VERMILION, 2002.

Sharp, Kerri (ed.). *The Black Lace Book of Women's Sexual Fantasies*. LONDON: VIRGIN BOOKS, 2003.

Index